PENGUIN BOOKS
THE PERILS OF BEING MODERATELY FAMOUS

Soha Ali Khan is an Indian film actor who has appeared in movies such as *Rang De Basanti*, *Tum Mile*, *Khoya Khoya Chand* and *Sahib Biwi Aur Gangster Returns*. She studied modern history at Balliol College, Oxford, and earned a masters' degree in international relations from the London School of Economics and Political Science. She is the youngest daughter of actor Sharmila Tagore and Mansoor Ali Khan Pataudi, the ninth nawab of Pataudi. Both her father and paternal grandfather, Iftikhar Ali Khan Pataudi, were former captains of the Indian cricket team. Her older brother is Saif Ali Khan and she's married to actor Kunal Khemu.

the perils of being moderately famous

SOHA ALI KHAN

PENGUIN BOOKS

An imprint of Penguin Random House

PENGUIN BOOKS

USA | Canada | UK | Ireland | Australia
New Zealand | India | South Africa | China

Penguin Books is part of the Penguin Random House group of companies
whose addresses can be found at global.penguinrandomhouse.com

Published by Penguin Random House India Pvt. Ltd
7th Floor, Infinity Tower C, DLF Cyber City,
Gurgaon 122 002, Haryana, India

First published in Penguin Books by Penguin Random House India 2017

Excerpts in Chapter 1 'Big Shoes, Small Feet' reproduced from *Pataudi: Nawab
of Cricket* with permission from HarperCollins Publishers India

ISBN 9780143439967

Typeset in Baskerville by Manipal Digital Systems, Manipal
Printed at Thomson Press India Ltd, New Delhi

www.penguin.co.in

To my daughter, Inaaya

Contents

Introduction

If you have bought/borrowed/shoplifted this book in the hopes of finding out the secret behind Kareena's glowing complexion or what Bhai really meant when he talked about the difference between nepotism and eugenics then, unfortunately, this is not the book for you.

Although in the ensuing pages there may be a passing reference to some of the idiosyncrasies of the more famous members of my family, the bulk of it, I'm afraid, is about . . . well, me.

Just me.

Is my life really worth writing about or, more to the point, worth your paying to read about? Well, the good news is you were right not to wait for the movie.

The truth of the matter is I have some time on my hands. By the time this book comes out I'll be thirty-nine—unless books are like some of my movies and have gestation periods longer than those of alpine salamanders (48 months). See, you have learnt something already, albeit of questionable practical relevance unless you happen to stumble into a convention on herpetology.

But I digress. As a female actor who has been in the industry for over twelve years and who, as I said earlier, is on the wrong side of her thirties, satisfying roles in films are about as rare as a pothole-free Mumbai highway during the monsoon. You see, as a woman in commercial films, you can either be the love interest of the hero or the mother of the hero and for that you need to be playing someone under thirty or over fifty respectively.

So what does a female actor in her forties do? Open a production company. Set up a jewellery designing business. Become an interior decorator. Start a family. Launch a fashion line. Write a book.

My friends will tell you I dress well and have a keen sense of style, but my best friends will tell you that I find dressing up a daunting experience. I can choose an outfit, but I will readily admit that matching shoes, bag, jewellery, lipstick, nail polish and a complementary hairstyle is beyond me. I can finish a cryptic crossword in less time than I would take to get myself ready for a red-carpet event. The same goes for interior decoration or jewellery designing, thereby eliminating most of my options for self-employment in the coming decade. As for the first option—open a production company—Kunal and I have already done that; it's called Renegade Films and we hope to produce some exciting content under its banner but that takes time. And so, as I said before, I have some time on my hands.

Start a family—hmmm, now this is a tricky one. Which comes first—the chicken or the egg? The nesting or the baby? Because I don't feel it right now—that maternal yearning. I went to my gynaecologist the other day to ask how late was too late to have a baby.

'I don't smoke, I don't drink, I do yoga and play badminton, and everyone says I look much younger than I am,' I warbled on, singing my own praises.

Her response was short and brutal. 'Your ovaries can't see your face.' Something to think about.

Write a book. If I had a dollar for every person who has said that to me, I would have ... ummm ... six dollars. 'You are so intelligent', 'You went to Oxford', 'You read so many books'. Surely it takes more than that? To write a book, don't you need a story to tell? A story worth telling?

So let's start at the beginning and see where we end up.

Big Shoes, Small Feet

'Are you famous?'

It wasn't the first time I had been asked that question (and it probably won't be the last), but I have always struggled with the right answer.

I was in Selfridges, the well-known Oxford Street department store that has become a social landmark in London. It was July, 2015, and the much-anticipated summer sale had just kicked off which meant the store was teeming with people. I had managed to get my hands on Charlotte Tilbury's 'Pillow Talk' lip liner, indisputably the luxury launch of the decade, which promised the perfect shade of nude so that your lips appeared bare of make-up altogether.

As I was waiting in line to pay the sixteen pounds you couldn't convince me for the world I was throwing away, an Indian girl at the cosmetic counter recognized my face and called out to her friends. Soon a decent-sized group had formed around me, asking for selfies. Some of the non-Indian people also stopped to look.

'Are you famous?' asked the saleswoman as I got to the front of the queue to pay for my shopping.

I glanced at the name tag on the saleswoman's shirt.

'Well, Becky, not if you have to ask,' I quipped, but inside I was feeling an odd mix of embarrassment and self-importance.

'Who is she?' I heard her ask one of the gaggle of giggling girls as I turned to leave.

'Don't you know?' the girl gasped.

I smiled at her response, feeling quite pleased with myself. I had only recently become active on social media and my Instagram account was gaining in popularity with followers from the UAE and England as well as other parts of the world.

'She's Saif Ali Khan's sister!'

I closed my eyes momentarily as irritation gave way to submission. Of course! And it was true. I was. I am.

It's probably safe to say I have been recognized as Sharmila Tagore's daughter or Saif Ali Khan's sister more times than I have been recognized as Soha Ali Khan. You would think it would get irksome but I have learnt, over time, to embrace that part of my identity.

Are you famous?—It's a good question, one that I have often been asked and one that I frequently ask myself. I would say I am 'moderately famous'. People in India, and some outside of India, know who I am. What does that mean?

What it doesn't mean is that they always know my name. They will stop in the street and point me out to their companions (this happens often). Some have seen my films and do know me, and some are fans of my brother, Saif (Bhai), my sister-in-law, Kareena, my mother, Sharmila Tagore (Amman), or my father, Mansur Ali Khan Pataudi (Abba), and recognize me as the youngest member of a somewhat notable family. I am not competing with my family members nor am I jostling for my place in the sun. I am content to bask in reflected glory whilst seeking out my unique destiny.

This book is my tribute to my family, without whom I would not be here. Without whom I would not be who I am. It seems only fitting then to begin with them, to delve into a history that is as splendid and illustrious as it is anachronistic and eccentric. In writing about them I wonder if my life is relatable

It's hard work being a Fairy Princess

to most. The bulk of my experiences have been somewhat different, if not unique. I am, after all, a princess. Now try not to imagine me saying that while stomping my feet in a silver sequinned dress with a tiara on my head.

Had the privy purses and princely titles not been abolished in 1971, my official title would have been Nawabzadi Soha Ali Khan of Pataudi and Bhopal.

~

Pataudi, Bhopal

Pataudi Palace, circa 2006

It may come as a surprise to some of you that Pataudi is not a name but a place. It is a small town in the state of Haryana with a grand total of approximately 23,000 people. It has been ruled by nawabs since 1804 when it was founded by the East India Company as a reward to Faiz Talab Khan for his help against the Maratha Empire in the Second Anglo-Maratha War.

The eighth nawab was my paternal grandfather, Iftikhar Ali Khan Pataudi, more famous for playing cricket for both India and England and for later captaining the Indian cricket team. He went to the same college I would attend almost seventy years later—Balliol College, Oxford University, where he won a Blue for cricket and for hockey. A Blue is an award given to athletes at Oxford or Cambridge University and some other colleges for competition at the highest level. If you are awarded a Blue it means that you have displayed consistent skill in a particular sport at an international or world-class level. The only Blue I came close to during my time at Oxford was the hue my skin took on from December to February!

Sarkar Abba, as he was known to us, had full legal jurisdiction over the people—as long as he did not contradict British policy—until he signed the Instrument of Accession in 1947 when the British Raj ended and Pataudi became a part of the Republic of India.

Sarkar Abba, looking sharp

I once asked my father why Sarkar Abba had elected to stay in India when so many of his family members, such as his younger brother Sher Ali Khan Pataudi and his cousin Sahabzada Yaqub Ali Khan, chose to move to Pakistan after Partition. As a well-read and discerning member of the Muslim aristocracy, he would have secured a high-ranking position in the new Pakistan government. Sher Ali Khan, due to his prior military experience in the Indian Armed Forces, was appointed adjutant general of the Pakistan Army and later served as the chief of general staff; Yaqub Khan rose through the ranks of the foreign service to become ambassador to the United States and subsequently foreign minister in 1982. Instead Sarkar Abba chose to stay on in Hindu-majority India amidst tremendous upheaval, relinquishing his kingdom in return for a privy purse of a mere Rs 48,000 per annum. 'He didn't believe in the idea of Pakistan,' Abba told me—a country built on a foundation of religion. Sarkar Abba and my grandmother decided to stand with the new nation state of India and the democratic and secular ideals it stood for.

My paternal grandmother, Sajida Sultan—Badi Amman, as we called her—was the second daughter of Nawab Hamidullah Khan, the last ruling nawab of Bhopal. In the absence of a male heir in direct line of succession, her elder sister, Abida Sultan, should have inherited the throne but when Abida chose to leave for

Pakistan after Partition she relinquished this right to her younger sister.

There may have been male contenders for the title from less direct branches of the family tree, but Badi Amman's grandmother, Nawab Sultan Jehan Begum, one of the greatest rulers of Bhopal, was behind the decision of the British Viceroy to declare Abida the heir apparent. This was at a time when Nawab Hamidullah himself was only thirty years old and his wife, twenty-five—they could still have had more children, perhaps a son.

But Sultan Jehan was resolute in her decision: Successive women rulers had effectively governed Bhopal for over 107 years, proving that there was no difference between a male and a female leader and therefore the eldest child, irrespective of gender, would be recognized as the heir. Provided, of course, that they were fit to rule, which she ensured under her able tutelage that all three of her granddaughters would be.

Ten-year-old Sajida Sultan's daily routine was thus:

5 a.m. to 6 a.m.: Open-air exercise

6 a.m. to 7 a.m.: Morning meal

8 a.m. to 10 a.m.: Reading of the Quran

10 a.m. to 11 a.m.: Breakfast with Nawab Sultan Jehan Begum

11 a.m. to 12 noon: Recreation

Badi Amman (left), age 6, with her sisters

12 noon to 1 p.m.: Handwriting lesson

2 p.m. to 3 p.m.: English lesson

3 p.m. to 4 p.m.: Persian lesson

4 p.m. to 5 p.m.: Arithmetic lesson

5 p.m. to 5.30 p.m.: Pashtu/fencing lessons alternately

5.30 p.m. to 6.30 p.m.: Riding/swimming lessons
alternately

6.30 p.m. to 7 p.m.: Evening meal

8 p.m.: Bed

Having read and marvelled at this schedule in *The Begums
of Bhopal* by Shahryar M. Khan, Abida Sultan's son and
Abba's cousin, whom we call Mian Huzoor, I cannot

resist the temptation to share my own daily routine (on a non-working day) which, as you will surmise, varies somewhat from Badi Amman's in content and concentration:

10 a.m.: Alarm goes off

10 a.m. to 10.40 a.m.: Snooze (x4)

10.45 a.m. to 11.30 a.m.: Drink coffee whilst scrolling through Instagram feed

11.30 a.m.: Make impossible choice of whether to eat breakfast or simply wait an hour for lunch

12 noon to 1 p.m.: Yoga/gym alternately

1 p.m. to 1.30 p.m.: Lunch

1.30 p.m. to 2.30 p.m.: Get updates from Twitter on national news and from Ninna on 'local news'

3 p.m. to 5 p.m.: Browse through Netflix/Hotstar/Amazon in search of content appropriate for daytime viewing, such as light comedic entertainment along the lines of *Rake* or *The Royals*

5 p.m.: Stare into fridge hoping something delicious and healthy will miraculously materialize, failing which think about what to order from Scootsy (an online food delivery service) for an evening snack

6 p.m. to 7 p.m.: Bonding time with Masti (our nine-year-old Beagle) which involves my throwing a ball and then ultimately having to retrieve it myself

8 p.m. onwards: Browse through Netflix/Hotstar/
Amazon in search of content appropriate for night-
time viewing, such as dark drama or thrillers along the
lines of *Line of Duty* or *The Making of a Murderer*
12 midnight to 1 a.m.: Bedtime reading (current book
of choice being *A Little Life* by Hanya Yanagihara)

If you are impressed with my indolence on a holiday,
I should point out that on the days I am working it is
possible to end up doing even less. As an actor it is a well-
accepted fact that you are paid handsomely not to act,
but to wait. Sometimes for hours on end whilst elaborate
shots are being set up, another actor's close-ups are being
taken or the lead actor takes a five-hour nap in his trailer.

Coming back to the point, when Hamidullah Khan
passed away in 1960, the Government of India recognized
Badi Amman as the Nawab Begum of Bhopal.

Bhopal was India's largest Muslim-ruled princely
state after Hyderabad, with a population of one million
and a nineteen-gun salute. Pataudi, in comparison, was a
non-salute collective of villages.

It is said that when he learnt of Sarkar Abba's and
Badi Amman's romance and their desire to marry, Nawab
Hamidullah was not exactly jubilant about this match of
'unequals' and refused to sanction the union. It was only
when Badi Amman was literally dying of heartache (and

perhaps some tuberculosis) that her elder sister intervened and took on their unyielding father. She is said to have stormed into his office and demanded to know why an affable and aristocratic nawab, both educated and renowned, was not good enough for his daughter.

Hitched at last

Unable to provide a justifiable response, Hamidullah gave his consent, albeit unwillingly.

Some suspect his reluctance stemmed from a sportsman's jealousy. Nawab Hamidullah Khan was a

Nawab Hamidullah Khan, casual Friday

nine-goal-handicap polo player. For those of you unfamiliar with the sport, players are rated on a scale from minus 2 to 10 where minus 2 indicates a novice player and 10 is the highest handicap possible. There are less than two dozen ten-handicap polo players in the world today and all but one are Argentine! Hamidullah Khan was also an excellent shot and a competent wrestler but it was Sarkar Abba who stole the limelight: in polo, hockey and cricket, among other sports.

The much-in-love couple were finally married in April 1939. Since then there has been a robust tradition of marrying for love and love alone in our family—which my father upheld by marrying a Hindu actress in 1968, my brother by marrying someone outside of his religion and a good few years older than him at the very young age of twenty in 1990 and then again someone a good few years younger than him in 2012, and yours truly by marrying a young Hindu actor with a twinkle in his eye and a lopsided grin in 2015.

I never met Sarkar Abba—he died at the young age of forty-two. It was 5 January 1952, my father's eleventh birthday. My father and his school friends were all playing musical chairs at home, waiting for Sarkar Abba and Badi Amman to return from the Jaipur Polo Ground. The cake would be cut and refreshments served after they arrived. But Sarkar Abba never came home. He died of a massive heart attack, falling from his horse halfway through the second chukka of the polo match in front of a stunned crowd. It could have been the result of years of chain-smoking—I suspect Abba was inclined to think as much because he himself gave up the habit a month before his forty-second birthday. Abba never got around to cutting the cake that day, and he never celebrated his birthday again.

In the lap of luxury

I cannot imagine what it must have been like to lose your father at such a young age but I do know what it is like to lose your father before time. To write even a few words about him seems an impossible task because I feel my words will not do justice to how I feel about him, that they will fall short of conveying what he meant to me. So let's first agree that words do not suffice.

I've always thought Abba's story should be told. Even when he was alive I would often ask him if he was going to write an autobiography. 'The truth can never be told,' he liked to say mysteriously, 'and I will not lie.' I soon gave up trying to figure out what he meant—he liked to speak in code—I suspect in order to deter conversation as much as possible, except for the very persistent. I did not persist then but after he passed away I have learnt so much more about him—from obituaries, personal stories, letters written to my mother from friends, colleagues and admirers. I have wallowed in those words of tribute and praise and felt privileged to be loved so dearly by one loved dearly by so many.

The Tiger in his den

My strongest memories of Abba are all lying down—his favourite place in the world was at home in his den in front of the picture window overlooking the trees and birds, propped up on a *gau-takiya* reading a book and having his feet pressed by Gyaasuddin, his loyal man Friday.

Whilst my mother, my brother, my sister and I travelled the world making films and speeches, giving and receiving awards, caught up in hectic schedules, you could always count on him to be at home by the landline, solid and dependable as a rock. He had a love-hate relationship with the phone—insisting on sitting practically on top of it and yet frustrated by the sound of it ringing. As a sixteen-year-old teenage girl you can only imagine how mortifying it was to have your friends call home asking to speak to you and for the grouchy man on the other end to hang up on them with a curt 'no'. His ownership over the single landline with the infinitely long extension cord continued even after he went to bed with the fastening of a lock on the dial pad. He had an incredible vocabulary but he didn't believe in wasting words—and so it was to be for us!

A typical conversation with him went like this:

Me (calling from university in England): Aadaab, Abba. How are you?
Him: Who's that?
Me: Umm, it's Soha, Abba.
Him: Your mother's not home.
Me: Oh, that's okay, but how are you?
Him: Fine. I'll tell her you called.
Me: Okay, Abba. Ummm . . .
Him: Are you okay for money?
Me: Yes. (As if I'd tell him if I wasn't!)
Click.

His frugality with words was exercised in other areas too. People often ask me what it was like to grow up in a royal household and I never know what to say . . . You imagine a life abundant in riches and indulgences—someone pressing your feet first thing in the morning and last thing at night, a chauffeur at your disposal and handmaidens to comb your hair and lay out your freshly laundered clothes, and yes we did have all of this and more, but you must believe me when I say that there was never really a sense of being flush with wealth—quite the contrary. Abba was an economical man. He didn't own imported cars, except the one distinctive white Jaguar two-seater with the licence plate PAT1, and he never bought expensive designer brands.

Abba's most prized possession, after us of course!

When he went shopping in London to replace a pair of socks he would buy just that, turning a blind eye (pardon the pun) to all other consumerist temptations. He bought only what he needed and didn't seem to really want anything. He was careful with money. Our doors and various tabletops at home would be covered in yellow Post-it notes, his signature scrawl barely legible but you could just about make out the four words: 'Turn the lights off.' He didn't like to waste petrol. If we wanted the car to go to a friend's house my sister and I had to think very carefully about how to approach the subject.

Wrong approach: 'Abba, may I please use the car to go to Khan Market?' That would lead to his favourite word: 'No.'

Right approach: 'Abba, have you read (insert some new article or book on history or politics—or in later years an even better distraction was a wildlife video on YouTube) . . . oh and (to be tossed in as breezily as possible) I'm going to Priyanka's for dinner; I'll be back in a couple of hours.' Followed by a swift exit.

Perhaps it was a sense of financial insecurity that led him to this conservation, having lost so much becoming Mr Khan. In fact loss was no stranger to him—losing his father at the age of eleven, the sight in his right eye at twenty, his titles and privy purses at thirty. Of course all of those things happened well before I came on the scene, but I remember the move from a sprawling three-acre bungalow at 1, Dupleix Road (renamed K. Kamraj Marg around the same time Connaught Place's inner circle was renamed Rajiv Gandhi Chowk) to the more modest home in Vasant Vihar.

Whilst the rest of us may have complained—Amman about losing her rose bushes and jamun trees, my sister about having to climb two flights of stairs to get to her room, me about not having a badminton court in our backyard—Abba was quick to adjust. He was always quick to adjust and was as comfortable in the palace in Pataudi as he was in my poky two-bedroom flat in Bandra. As long as his clothes were pressed and a good book to read produced come 10 p.m., he would look after himself, even making his own morning tea and always remembering to turn the lights off!

It could have been because he had seen so much loss in his life or perhaps it was his character-building boarding school education, but Abba knew the value of money and I would like to think that those lessons in the importance of saving have trickled down to me.

Abba didn't like to talk about the setbacks in his life. If I asked him about his father he would say he didn't remember him very much. If I asked about his eye, he would brush it off as 'a bit of bad luck'. I had to discover in articles and from friends just how brilliant a batsman he was before the injury. He had already earned himself a bit of a reputation in school as a natural cricketer, graceful and lightning quick in the field. In fact Badi Amman decided to employ the English professional cricketer, Frank Woolley, who had been Sarkar Abba's coach to train Abba when he was only twelve. She

Swag

would attend each of these coaching classes and watch attentively from afar. She soon noticed that for the most part Woolley was just standing to the side watching Abba practise in the nets. After multiple sessions of much the same, she finally went up to him to gently remind him that he was being paid handsomely for his instruction. Woolley looked at her and simply said, 'I wouldn't change anything. I wouldn't change anything at all.'

Cricketing enthusiasts will recall the name of Douglas Jardine, captain of the English team during the 1932–33 Ashes tour of Australia. Under him England employed the controversial bodyline tactic against Australian batsmen wherein bowlers pitched the ball short on the line of leg stump to rise towards the bodies of batsmen in a way that was aggressive and also potentially dangerous.

Jardine became very unpopular with the Australians who booed him repeatedly for this tactic from the stands. Sarkar Abba had been selected to play on the English squad then and was one of the only players to indicate his disapproval by refusing to take up his leg-side fielding position. Jardine is known to have declared, 'I see His Highness is a conscientious objector,' and promptly dropped him from the team.

Towards the end of the tour, Sarkar Abba said of Jardine: 'I am told he has his good points. In three months I have yet to see them.' I bring up this story because many years later, in 1959, a young student at Winchester, aged eighteen, finally broke Douglas Jardine's long-standing school record of 997 runs in a season. That young student was none other than my father; the son had avenged his father's honour—it's the stuff movies are made of! Incidentally Abba's record of 1068 runs stood for fifty-six years until it was broken by a young English student named Dan Escott in 2015.

I used to love hearing about Abba's favourite cricket moments, one of the earliest being the 1960 Oxford vs Cambridge Blues match, a first-class game (three or more days with two innings played by each team) held at Lord's in London. In today's age of Twenty20 cricket, varsity matches are a bit of an anachronism but in the 1960s there was no better place for a student cricketer than

Oxford or Cambridge. If you scored runs or took wickets at the Parks, the home ground of the Oxford University Cricket Club, you would be noticed and wooed by the counties. And to play at Lord's has always been special— even before India defeated England in the NatWest final in July 2002 and skipper Sourav Ganguly, watching from the balcony, took his shirt off to celebrate! I myself have walked from the dressing room through the Long Room, down the stairs and on to the Ground—this was on the occasion of the Memorial Dinner that was held for Abba in the Long Room in the summer of 2012 when Charles Fry, an English former first-class cricketer friend of Abba's, kindly agreed to take Kunal and me on a tour. I can only imagine what Abba must have felt making that same walk to the expectant gaze of the crowds.

His own father had scored a century in his first varsity match and expectations from Abba, buttressed by his school exploits, were high. It was 7 July 1960. Cambridge had been bowled out quickly for 153 and Oxford stood at a shaky 32 for 3 when he came in to bat as he often did at number 5. Abba scored 131 runs. It was always special to him, his first first-class century at Lord's. He could finally silence those who were so eager to say of famous sons of famous fathers, 'He'll never be as good as his father.'

Then there was the innings against fierce Fred Trueman at the Parks in 1961 where he scored 106 against an invincible Yorkshire team. It must have done considerable repair to a collectively bruised national pride to score a century against the same man who had put the humiliating score of 0 for 4 during the 1952 Test series against India—four wickets taken and not a single run scored! In 1961 he was only 92 runs short of breaking the university record of 1307 runs in a season with three games left to play when the accident happened.

It was so avoidable. Oxford University, of which Abba had been unanimously chosen as captain post his century at Lord's, was playing Sussex County. At the end of play on the first day, Oxford had scored only 4 runs and lost both openers. A few of the players decided to go out for dinner that night; Robin Waters drove them in his Morris 1000. After dinner some wanted to walk back and so Abba hopped in the front passenger seat to keep Robin company. They were still parked when, without any warning, they were hit hard by a passing car, sending Abba flying through the windscreen, shattering the glass. He hadn't even had the chance to put his seat belt on.

Everyone was shaken up of course but the damage seemed to be limited to Abba's right hand—he feared he had broken his wrist and was worried he wouldn't be able to play the next day. It was only much later, at Brighton Hospital, that they discovered the shard of glass in his right eye.

Emergency surgery could not repair the dissolved lens and Abba was left with merely 5 per cent vision in that eye.

Can you imagine how difficult it is to play any sport with one eye? Try this at home. Cover one eye with a hand and try pouring water into a glass. It's not so easy. You need both eyes to judge distance. And that's a stationary object. Now imagine standing at the crease and facing bowlers the likes of West Indies' Andy Roberts, one of the four horsemen of the apocalypse, bowling at you at 200 kilometres an hour. Abba told me that once, as he was walking in to bat, he passed the wicketkeeper who was crouching closer to the boundary than to the crease.

'What are you doing all the way back here?' Abba asked him.

'You're about to find out, man,' was the bone-chilling reply.

Charlie Griffith was bowling. Griffith, as some of you may know, was the West Indian fast bowler with an arguably lethal chucking style responsible for prematurely ending Nari Contractor's cricket career. It was the 1962 Indian tour of the West Indies and Nari Contractor was captain; a twenty-one-year-old Tiger Pataudi, still raw from the eye accident, was vice-captain. This was a time that preceded the full battle armour of helmets, abdominal guards, thigh guards, chest guards and arm guards our cricketers wear today. When the ball hit Contractor on the side of the head the crack was so loud that Abba swore he heard it all the way in the dressing room. With blood pouring from his ears and nose, Contractor walked off the pitch, leaving the groundsmen to soak up as much of it off the crease as they could using pails of sawdust. Multiple surgeries removed the blood clots from his brain and saved his life, but Contractor would never play Test cricket again. Abba was abruptly thrust into an early captaincy many felt he was unprepared for.

Having only recently lost vision in his right eye, Abba may not have fared so well against the likes of Wes Hall and Charlie Griffith in 1962 but he would get the opportunity to strike back in 1974–75 when the West Indies team toured India under Clive Lloyd's captaincy. The West Indies had won the first two matches and were in full attack mode as the sun rose over Eden Gardens in Calcutta on 27 December 1974. It was early in the game when a bouncer from Andy Roberts hit Abba squarely in the jaw, shattering the bone and the hopes of the

Down but not out; Abba leaving the ground with a broken jaw

1,00,000 Indians in the stadium. Not one to be deterred so easily, Abba had his jaw wired up and was back to resume his wicket, going on to hit Vanburn Holder for four consecutive boundaries in one over! India won the match by 85 runs—a historic victory that, even today, remains one of our most iconic Test triumphs.

The car accident must have crushed him at the time but he was a fighter. 'I lost sight in one eye,' he said, 'but I didn't lose sight of my ambition.'

He had already seen the life he wanted to live and he refused to let it become an impossible dream. If there is ever a story of following your dreams, against the odds, his is it. How he did it and the details of his cricketing genius are subjects for another book, but anything I write about myself is incomplete without writing about him. He was, by far, the most effortlessly cool man I have ever met—astute, judicious and quick-witted.

I remember reading out questions to him from my Australian visa application form. 'Have you ever been convicted of a crime?' the form asked.

'Write "I didn't think it was still necessary!"' he said to me, chuckling gleefully. He was referring, of course, to Australia's history as a penal colony used by the British government to deal with the overcrowding of their own prisons.

Abba would giggle often, going bright red in the face—usually whilst watching his favourite television shows *Fawlty Towers* and *Allo Allo*.

Life is just better when you're laughing

By the time I was born my father had retired from professional cricket, so I never got the chance to see him play. It was only when he was in the hospital that I saw that fighting spirit people had spoken of; I saw my father the athlete. In the three weeks he spent in the hospital the steroids ate away more than half of his muscle tone but his heart was inexhaustible. The ICU doctors said they'd never seen anything like it. And we were so proud of him, so proud to be his chosen ones.

Even there, surrounded by tubes, masks, drips, pills, syringes and doctors, he didn't want a fuss. He was always polite, ever-charming—asking every technician a question about their home village or city; making them feel comfortable even through his discomfort. Through him I have seen how a good leader commands, doesn't demand respect; not once raising his voice—at most a plaintive 'Rinkoo . . .'* if my mother's tone was especially penetrating (a not uncommon occurrence).

Through Abba I have learnt tolerance and a live-and-let-live attitude.

Tradition mattered, respect for one's elders mattered, but not for their own sake—and if there was ever a clash with what he wanted, he was not to be confined by custom. That in particular I am grateful for, for it led to my parents' happy marriage against the wishes of many— the reputation of nawabs and actors being equally suspect in the sixties—and so to me!

---

* Rinkoo is Amman's 'daak naam'—a Bengali always has two names: a 'bhalo naam' of the 'what is your good name' fame and a deeply embarrassing 'daak naam' or pet name. For instance, we all know the President of India at the time of writing as the Hon'ble Pranab Mukherjee but to his family and friends he will always be Poltu!

On 5 January 2011 we celebrated his seventieth birthday in Pataudi. He never celebrated his birthday, having lost his father on that same day, at the age of eleven, but somehow that year my mother insisted, and somehow that year he relented. And so, surrounded by his closest friends and family, we ate, drank, told stories, recited poems, had a magic show and screened a short film we made for him . . . He rolled his eyes at all the fuss but I know he loved it.

A rare picture of the whole family; by rare
I mean the ONLY one

As a family, we're not big on public demonstrations of affection but we wanted to show him how much we all love him, really spell it out for a change, and I am so thankful that we were given the chance to do that before he was taken from us so swiftly a mere eight months later. He was too young to go, of course, and there was nothing really wrong with him, except his lungs wouldn't function—an incurable, irreversible disease called Idiopathic Pulmonary Fibrosis—there was no rationalizing it, no hope of fighting it. The only real way for us to deal with his death, the ultimate setback, has been to take it on the chin as he always did—'a bit of bad luck'.

On 22 September 2011 at 5.55 p.m., with his whole family at his side, Abba breathed his last. I was holding his hand when he went and I could see his heartbeat start to fall on the monitor, slowly at first and then more rapidly. He was tired. Every movement for him was like running a marathon; and it was time to stop. It is very hard to deal with the loss of a parent, especially when it is untimely, but if there is something that Abba's life has taught me, it is acceptance. Life will knock you down time and time again, and you must find the strength inside you to stand up. Never give up the fight—not until your dying breath.

When we are at Pataudi I like to take a book and go sit by his grave, where he lies silently, surrounded by trees and the birds chirping.

Abba's final resting place

My world has changed, but there it seems things are not so different. We talk to each other, he and I—I say a lot more than he does; I always have . . . and he remains in death as he always was through life, my rock.

2

Bangla Bolte Paro?

THE TAGORE FAMILY TREE

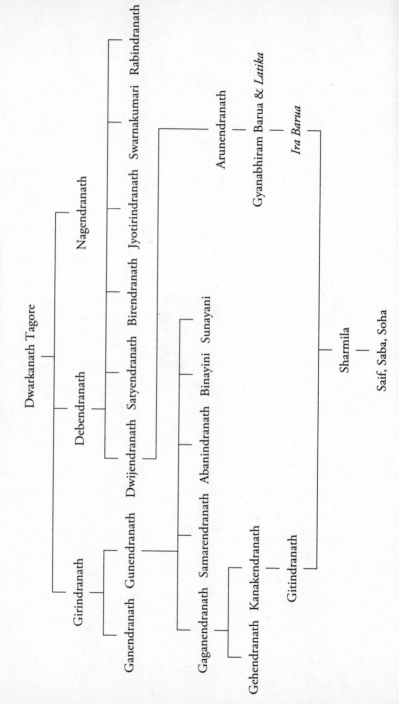

The first time I attended a press conference in Kolkata, a journalist kept referring to Amman as Sharmila Thakur. I let it go once, twice even, but finally I felt compelled to correct her. 'My mother's name is not Thakur,' I explained kindly, 'it's Tagore.' The woman looked at me as if I were joking and then as if I were mad. Back at the hotel my manager broke it to me that Tagore is the anglicized version of Thakur, just as Chatterjee is of Chattopadhyay or Bose is of Basu.

I am half Bengali and Bangla is my mother tongue but I am afraid I do not speak it very well. Or at all, really. I have learnt a few lines to appease the local media when I visit West Bengal during Durga Pujo, for an event or a film promotion. But in spite of my linguistic limitations, it would be unjust not to devote some part of this book to the maternal side of my family. If my fame pales in comparison to the begums and nawabs who pepper the paternal side of my pedigreed ancestry, my mother's maiden name is no less daunting in its celebrity—Tagore.

The Tagore family has been one of the leading families of Calcutta for hundreds of years, rising to prominence during the Bengal Renaissance in the nineteenth century. The family has produced several notable personalities in various fields of art, the most famous being Rabindranath Tagore, the first non-European to win the Nobel Prize in Literature in 1913 and the only writer to have penned the national anthems of two countries—India, of course, and neighbouring Bangladesh. There is some confusion as to how exactly my mother is related to Rabindranath Tagore. I wanted to clarify the connection in this chapter and so I called up my mother to better understand. This is how our conversation went:

> Me: Amman, how exactly are you related to Rabindranath Tagore?
>
> Amman (taking a deep breath and launching forth): Dwarkanath Tagore had three sons, one of whom was Girindranath Tagore and one who was Debendranath Tagore. Debendranath had fourteen children (!!!), his penultimate child being Rabindranath Tagore. Girindranath (perhaps more aware of the population crisis which his brother was partially responsible for and seemed oblivious to!) had two sons: Ganendra and Gunendra. Gunendra had three sons: Gaganendra,

Samarendra and Abanindra. Gaganendra had a son
called Gitindranath, your Dada, my father . . .
Me: I'll have to call you back. With a pen. And lots
of paper.

And I thought it was silly of my parents to give us four-
letter names starting with S—Saif, Saba, Soha!

After much name-dropping I figured it out. My
mother's paternal great-grandfather was Gaganendranath
Tagore, Rabindranath Tagore's nephew. Gaganendranath
himself was an influential artist who studied and
assimilated Japanese brush techniques and the influence
of Far Eastern art into his own work. He then went on
to develop a post-modern style and was responsible for
bringing Cubism, considered by many to be the most
influential art movement of the twentieth century, to
India. But it is the connection with Rabindranath Tagore,
or Robi Da as he was called by those close to him, that is
most celebrated.

It is from my maternal grandmother, Ira Tagore,
that I learnt about Robi Da. She adored him. She told us
how she first met him in 1933 at Jorasanko, the Tagore
ancestral home, where he was performing one of his
dance dramas. He was seventy-two, she was thirteen and
completely in awe of him. Yet somehow she mustered up
the courage to approach him.

'What can I do for you?' she remembers him asking her. She shyly handed him her autograph book to sign, which he did. He then asked Lal Didi (we all called Amman's mother Lal Didi after the red bindi she always wore) to act in one of his plays. It wasn't much she told us, just a small non-speaking part—her first and last tryst with acting. Lal Didi met Robi Da a few times after that at family weddings and cultural events.

Robi Da loved eating *luchi*s as did Lal Didi, and so she would seek him out during mealtimes when he was sure to be served hot fluffy maida luchis which he would share with her. Post dinner he would retire to his room and all the children would fight over who got to press his legs.

It was on one of these evenings that Robi Da confessed to Lal Didi that he found her *pishi* Swarnalata (her father's elder sister) very beautiful and that he had wanted to marry her but because of her tainted background his father had not allowed it. Lal Didi's grandfather, Rai Bahadur Gunabhiram Barua, had married a widow after his first wife died and this second wife gave birth to Swarnalata. Hindu social conventions in those days forbade widow remarriage and so this union and any consequences of it were viewed with disapproval.

You would think Robi Da's father, Debendranath Tagore, one of the founders of the Brahmo Samaj, an enlightened soul and reformer of Hinduism, would not have paid heed to such an archaic custom but you'd be surprised. Lal Didi, all of thirteen and not one to let convention stand in her way, leapt at the opportunity.

'So what? I'll marry you!' she told Robi Da passionately. Robi Da, perhaps accustomed to girls proposing to him over the odd luchi, asked for her autograph book and wrote her this poem instead:

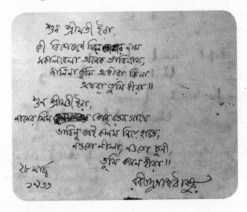

Shono Shrimati Ira
Kon bishoshon-e mile tomar naam
Shokal bela onek bhabhilam
Jani na tumi adhira ki na
Othoba tumi dheera

Shono Shrimati Ira
Naamer mil kon ratan shaathe
Bhabhiloom tai kolom niye haathe
Noy to neela noy to chuni
Tumi kamal heera

Translation:

> Listen Ira,
> All morning I have thought
> Of adjectives to define your name
> Are you impatient?
> Or are you tranquil?
>
> Listen Ira,
> Pen in hand I wonder
> Which jewel do I compare you to?
> Neither sapphire, nor ruby,
> You are a rare lotus diamond.

A few years later when Didi went to Santiniketan to study under Tagore's tutelage, he wrote her another poem:

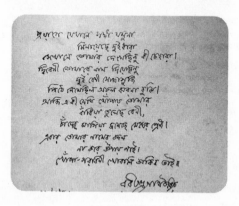

Prayag-e jekhane Ganga Jamnuna
Milayechhe dhara

Sekhane tomar dekhechhinu ki chehara.
Dwibeni tomar naam diyechhinu
Dui beni mukhomukhi
Peethe nemecchilo achal jharna bujhi.
Aaji e ki dekhi khopaye tomar
Badhiya tulechho beni,
Chander majhiya jomechhe megher shreni.
Ebar tomar naam badal
Na kore upay nai.
Khopa-garobini khobani dakibo tai.

Translation:

Where Ganga-Yamuna meet in Prayag
I saw your visage, haunting,
Named you Dwibeni
Two pleats cascading down your back
Like a waterfall in spate.

And today, I see
Your hair tied in a bun
Like dark clouds
Gathering around the moon.

This calls for a change of name
Shall I call you chignon-proud 'Khobani'

Many years later, in 1970, when my grandparents were
moving home in Calcutta from Belvedere Estate to

Niharika Building in Alipore Road, Lal Didi realized she had left her bangle box behind in the old house. She asked Dada, my maternal grandfather, to pick it

Santiniketan

up on his way back from the office. He did so the next day and as he handed over the brightly coloured box he told her that there were two tattered scraps of paper nestled among the bangles which he had done her the good service of tearing up and throwing away.

Lal Didi and Robi Da

I would give anything to see Lal Didi's face when she heard this! She must have turned as red as her bindi. The 'scraps of paper' were the precious first autograph by Rabindranath Tagore that she had lovingly kept for thirty-seven years and a letter from Jawaharlal Nehru! She could have killed him, she told us later.

Lal Didi was one of the most progressive thinkers in our family. She was liberal and funny and we all looked forward to her visits. Dada passed away in 1999, many years before her, and she must have been devastated to lose her life partner. When Sarkar Abba passed away, Badi Amman resolved to only wear white—I can only ever remember her wearing white saris or a white gharara. She shunned all colour, all adornments.

Lal Didi dressed to
the nines

Badi Amman (in the white sari)
and her peeps

I had assumed Lal Didi, coming from a Brahmin family, would do the same. But she did not. She continued to wake up early every morning to dress up in colourful silk saris, matching shoes and handbag to boot; she always wore lipstick and kajal and covered up every pesky grey hair with painstaking precision, even when she was in the ICU with a heart scare. The only thing she stopped wearing was the big red bindi, a sign of wedlock. She told Amman that Dada had loved the way she made an effort to dress up every day and he would not have wanted her to stop.

Lal Didi was not one to be swayed by the opinions of others. Even when she was a young girl in a family with three brothers, she managed to carve a path for herself. She was always interested in philosophy and psychology and wanted to pursue higher studies after her BA. In early-twentieth-century India women were not encouraged to pursue a college education and Lal Didi's maternal uncle, with whom she was sent to stay in Allahabad after her own mother died during the birth of Lal Didi's younger sister, thought a BA was more than sufficient for her. On 15 November, her birthday, Lal Didi's father wanted to give her a Benarasi sari as a present. The sari cost Rs 50. And in those days the fees for an MA were the same. Lal Didi appealed to her father to send her to Banaras Hindu University instead. Impressed by her steadfast focus he, being more liberal-minded than her uncle, decided to give her both but on the condition that she study privately since attending a co-educational college was out of the question. Once enrolled there was no money left for books and she had to borrow textbooks and reference material from those who could spare them.

The Graduate

Electricity had only just come to the main districts of Uttar Pradesh and her uncle would not allow her to keep the lights on to prepare for her exams. Undeterred, Lal Didi studied hard and when she passed her father told her how proud he was of her. In getting an MA in English she had managed to do what none of his sons had done.

When I think about my grandmother and her struggle to attain what I took to be my right—a tertiary educational qualification—I am inclined to believe the struggle for women's empowerment in India has progressed, if not in leaps and bounds then at least by a few meaningful steps for some of us.

My paternal great-grandmother was married at the age of nine and had her first child when she was thirteen, Lal Didi had to fight for her degree and Amman has been asked her whole life how her husband 'allowed' her to work. My life, in comparison, has been smooth sailing where at every stage I have enjoyed the privilege of choice—be it higher studies, occupation or life partner, and for this I am so grateful to my foremothers for paving the way!

My mother's side of the family has always been driven by intellectual and creative pursuits—Amman and her two younger sisters were also trained in dance and theatre from a young age. In 1956, at the age of five, Oindrila or Tinku Mashi (her 'daak naam'), was cast in the role of Mini in Tapan Sinha's *Kabuliwala* with Chhabi Biswas in the lead role. The film was based on a short story written by Rabindranath Tagore and it seemed appropriate that someone from his family play the role. Chinki Mashi, the youngest sister, was also offered a role in *36 Chowringhee Lane* by Aparna Sen which she turned down as she wasn't interested in films. Of the three, it was Amman who went on to become a celebrated movie star.

After seeing Tinku Mashi in *Kabuliwala*, Satyajit Ray came looking for her elder sister to cast in the role of Aparna in *Apur Sansar*, the World of Apu. At the time, most 'good' families did not allow their daughters to work in films but Ray felt that as this family had already permitted one daughter to act in a film they would be less likely to object. Even though Amman was only thirteen at the time, Dada said they had no objections to her acting in the film but would not take any responsibility for her acting abilities or lack thereof!

Still from *Apur Sansar*

The objection came from Mrs Das, the principal of the Diocesan school where Amman was studying. She was adamant: 'If Sharmila will act in films she cannot continue to study in this school,' was the ultimatum given. The reason: It would set a bad example for the rest of the students. Dada could not contain his indignation.

'We are that Tagore family which has broken all stereotypical practices. Our family was one of the first in Guwahati to allow widow remarriage,' he declared proudly. '*We* don't want our daughter studying in this school.' (He was referring of course to Rai Bahadur Gunabhiram, Lal Didi's grandfather who married a widow.)

Amman was enrolled into Loreto Convent, Asansol, the next day. *Apur Sansar* went on to become a huge success and Ray cast Amman in *Devi* the following year during the school summer holidays. She was offered more films after that, notably a role in the film *Kanchenjunga*, but had to turn them down because she had to sit for her senior Cambridge exams, which she passed with distinction.

The call from Bombay came in 1961. Shakti Samanta was making a film called *Kashmir Ki Kali* starring Shammi Kapoor and he wanted to cast Amman in the lead. Lal Didi and Dada had to think hard before letting her do this film; they understood this would mean a complete change of direction for her—commercial cinema, living in Bombay, not being able to go to college. When she finally signed the contract it was for two films together. One thing led to another and soon Amman was a successful Hindi film heroine. She was famous. Lal Didi would accompany her on outdoors to Kashmir and Nainital, among other places, and when she couldn't—like when she was expecting Chinki Mashi—one of Dada's sisters would go.

An Evening in Paris   *Swati*   *Apur Sansar*

Lal Didi happily confessed to us that she was most excited when Amman was shooting with Uttam Kumar. She had a 'massive crush' on him—her own words—and would arrive on set every day during the shooting of *Nayak* and stare at him until he became uncomfortable and moved out of sight.

Lal Didi embraced life and enjoyed every moment of it: She loved the company of young people—her grandchildren and their friends, and we in turn adored her. She loved her two watered-down whiskies every night. In fact, she told us it was her father-in-law who taught her which alcohol to drink, and that it was easier to stay within one's limits with whisky as opposed to other drinks.

She would make us laugh—like the time when she had to have an eye operation. I called her to ask her what had happened.

'I was watching *Salaam Namaste* in the theatre,' she said agitatedly. 'The heroine's voice was so shrill I dislocated my retina!'

She loved watching movies. Towards the end, when she was in hospital, and the promos of my film *Ahista Ahista* were being shown on TV, she kept saying that she wanted to be able to see it. She never could see the movie but she did watch all my other films, the good and the bad, and would call me to tell me her thoughts.

I remember watching Rituparno Ghosh's *Antarmahal* with her, a Bengali film set in nineteenth-century Calcutta where I play a repressed 'Chhoti Bahu'—wife to a wealthy zamindar intent on producing an heir. Attired as all Bengali women of that time period, I was wrapped in a sari without a blouse. The movie was commercially and critically acclaimed and my performance was well liked by most, but Lal Didi was insistent that I play no more of these blouse-less characters.

If Uttam Kumar was her crush in the 1960s then my grandmother's twenty-first-century crush was undoubtedly Aamir Khan. When I told her I had bagged a role in *Rang De Basanti* she said she wanted to come to the set to meet Aamir. We shot in Mumbai, Delhi, Jaipur and Punjab but sadly she was unable to come to any of the locations. However, in January 2006, when we were in Kolkata for film promotions, I asked Aamir if I could invite my grandmother to his hotel room to say hello. He kindly agreed. Lal Didi arrived beautifully turned out in a green silk sari the colour of bottled glass, her hair elegantly swept back into a neat bun at the nape of her neck. Aamir sat her down in a comfortable chair and asked her if she would like some tea or a fresh juice of some kind. Pat came the reply: 'Teacher's, no ice.' I bit back a smile at Aamir's look of surprise. It was 4 p.m.

If Lal Didi was liberal and independent in spirit, my Amman is much the same. At seventeen she was already living and working in Bombay. She was the first Indian actress to model a bikini on a magazine cover. At twenty-four, when her career was at its peak, she chose to commit what many called

The first dance

You can never be
overdressed or
overeducated

Two hearts and a diamond

professional hara-kiri, and got married—to a Muslim prince at that, at a time when inter-religious marriages were uncommon. She continued to work after marriage and well into motherhood; my brother was born two years after her marriage. In fact my childhood memories are of Abba being at home and Amman going to work—she would get us to wish her '10 on 10' as she was leaving.

I am the youngest of three. By the time I was born Amman was not working as much as she must have been when Bhai was young. I remember her being an active member of the school PTA, participating in bake sales and charity fundraisers. She would drop my sister and me off to school every morning until we reached that age when we are embarrassed by our parents and prefer them to stay a mile away from us in public.

There was even a time when she had chickenpox—which she got from me because I refused to stay away from her during the contagious phase—and I still insisted she come to school to drop me. Which she did, wrapped from head to toe in muslin and swooning from the fear of being discovered to be an irresponsible parent, exposing the children to pestilence. But apart from this one lapse of judgement, Amman continues to be the wisest and most sensible person I know. I have sought her advice on multiple occasions because I know she will not merely say what I want to hear but what I need to hear. From choice of boyfriend or college, to length of skirt and shape of eyebrow, I have always known where my mother stands. She is not exactly subtle with her opinions. Although not easy to digest, especially as a rebellious teenager, it would annoy me no end that ultimately she had the uncanny ability to always be right.

Hold the salute, I need to fix my hair

I think I've established by now that I have properly famous parents, and grandparents, and great-great-great-grand-uncles. My brother Saif, who I call Bhai, is also a famous movie star and he is married to Kareena Kapoor, one of Bollywood's most popular and successful actresses. Their son Taimur was trending on Twitter before he had even opened his eyes. Has all this celebrity had any impact on my life? I went to the same college as my father and saw his name in brass in the locker room of the Oxford University Parks Cricket Ground, right next to my grandfather's. I joined the same industry as my mother and brother

Like father like son

and have fought hard to carve my own identity within it. I am surrounded by my family's achievements. I am immensely proud of my heritage; I feel special to belong to this family that has so much history, so much talent and virtuosity running through its generations. I have benefited from my family connections—they have opened doors and facilitated introductions, provided me with a security and respect that I would otherwise have spent many years earning, given me recognition which brings a power that is not insignificant and afforded me financial security (that I try to keep at arm's length—like the boy you know you can depend on to take you to the ball when all else fails, but really you want Timothy to ask you. Timothy in this case is my own hard-earned money).

I remember going out for lunch with my family in Delhi as a child. Bhai had recently started working in films and his song 'Ole Ole' from *Yeh Dillagi* had become a big hit. Throughout the meal people kept coming to our table to ask for autographs—from my father, my mother and my brother. My sister and I could continue to eat our food undisturbed, which we rather enjoyed, feeling bad for the other three. I don't recall ever wanting to be as famous as them, wanting to sign autographs or having my hand shaken. I saw so much of it growing up that it didn't seem to retain much lustre.

I suspect the same is true of my sister, Saba. She has always been more comfortable behind the camera, taking beautiful pictures, than in front of it. Being of an artistic inclination, she chose to get her undergraduate degree from Delhi College of Arts, and then went to the

My big sis

Gemological Institute of America in Carlsbad, California, to study jewellery designing.

I chose to be a film actor, not for the fame or the money—I don't mean to sound arrogant when I say I had need of neither—but for the job, the creative fulfilment I get from walking in the shoes of another person. It was not, as many people assume, the easy choice to be an actor. In fact it was one of the most difficult decisions I have ever made. Since my first film in 2004 I have tried to carve out my own path, forge my own identity. I have achieved a level of success and fame that I can comfortably call my own, but that level is moderate in comparison to the accomplishments of my various family members. And therein lie the perils. Perils which, if you were made of flimsier stuff, would nibble away at you and leave you feeling less than whole.

As I said earlier, this book is my tribute to my family without whom I would not be here. Without whom I would not be who I am. With whom I have laughed and cried, opposed and obeyed, mourned and celebrated. With whom I have found the strength and support to grow, to discover who I am and who I am not. And with and without whom I am pursuing my happiness on my terms.

3

All Roads Lead to Saifeena

I was still lying in bed, scrolling through my Twitter feed, sipping coffee, more asleep than awake, when I saw the headline: Soha reveals major secret about Kareena Kapoor Khan's pregnancy.

What? When? Where? Who?

I couldn't answer any of the four basic questions journalists are taught to ask but I was already panicking—the coffee had turned to mud in my mouth and I was finding it difficult to breathe.

I am usually so careful, I never say anything about Amman, Bhai and Kareena—and especially nothing about the baby. Had I inadvertently let something slip?

I sat up and scanned the rest of the article and the more I read the more I relaxed. The major secret was that Bhai and Kareena, or Saifeena as they are together referred to, were not planning to have their child in London as far as I knew.

I remembered the interview. I remember answering the obligatory question about how I was feeling about becoming a *bua* again, dismissing the one about what preparations we were making, expressing vitriol over the one about whether I wanted a girl or a boy for them.

'Will they have the baby in London?' The question had come out of the blue and I was bemused.

'Why would they have the baby in London?' There was some furious scribbling and a furtive exchange of glances and I hastily added, 'I have no idea what they are planning and as far as I know they aren't planning to have the baby in London.' I ended with my most convincing but-what-would-I-know shrug.

So the fact that the baby would not be born in London—or Bolivia or Zimbabwe or Mars for that matter—was major news. Any tiny detail or non-detail is major news. And some journalists will come up with the most ingenious ways to uncover these titbits, as illustrated below by the line of questioning I am often subjected to:

Whilst premiering the first episode of *The Great Indian Home Makeover*—a televised show on interior redecorating that I host—

Q: Tell us about the show.

A: It's a home makeover show where we surprise a homeowner and make over one room in the space of forty-eight hours.

Q: Speaking of redecorating how are you doing up the baby's room in Saifeena's house?

Whilst at a press conference for Balmain watches—

Q: Tell us what you like about Balmain watches.

A: They are stylish, elegant and feminine. A woman's watch is more than just a timepiece, it's a piece of jewellery, a style accessory.

Q: Speaking of time, it's a happy time in the family with the baby coming. When is it due?

Whilst at a store inauguration for a jewellery brand—

Q: What is your favourite piece of jewellery?

A: My engagement ring, for obvious reasons.

Q: Speaking of rings, you will be ringing in the new year with a new family member, how will all of you spend New Year's Eve?

Whilst promoting the film *31st October*—

Q: Tell us about the film and your role in it.

A: It's a real-life story about the 1984 anti-Sikh riots and I play a Sardarni. I have three children in the film.

Q: Speaking of children . . . (Okay, this one I can forgive.)

Whilst at a Femina Diva style contest—

Q: What does style mean to you?

A: Wearing your personality on your sleeve, being comfortable, confident and carrying yourself in a way that makes you stand out.

Q: Speaking of standing out, isn't Kareena setting new fashion trends with her baby bump?

During a lifestyle interview—

Q: Where do you see yourself five years from now?

A: I don't plan ahead much—I try not to live in the past or plan for the future, I live in the present.

Q: Speaking of presents, what are you going to give the baby, have you decided?

During a press conference to announce Kunal and my production company Renegade Films—

Q: Why did you choose to name your company Renegade Films?

A: Renegade means rebel. We liked that it stands for going against the grain, doing things differently.

Q: Speaking of names, is it true they are naming the baby Saifeena?

You get the drift.

I calculated that the damage done in this instance was minimal, so I tossed my phone aside, took another sip of my coffee and turned to the less alarming headlines of the national press.

4

A Coming of Age

'Where are you going to college, Beta?' I remember an overly inquisitive aunty I didn't like very much asking me once. 'Balliol, Aunty,' was my somewhat pointed reply. She looked at me with obvious non-recognition and patted me on the head dismissively.

Balliol College, Oxford University. That would have impressed her, but I had decided by then that her opinion of me did not matter.

Balliol was founded in 1263 by John I de Balliol. It is one of the oldest colleges in Oxford, and in the English-speaking world. It also has the Lindsay Bar, the only fully student-run bar in the university, or at least it did when I was there. Among the college's alumni are three former British prime ministers—H.H. Asquith, Harold Macmillan and Edward Heath, five Nobel laureates, and a number of literary figures and philosophers, including Adam Smith, Robert Browning, Aldous Huxley and Graham Greene.

My personal favourites are evolutionary biologist Richard Dawkins and journalist Christopher Hitchens, otherwise known as 'The Hitch' who wrote a tell-all by that name: *Hitch-22*. If you look up Balliol College's notable alumni you will see a gallery of all these famous people, and among them, deservedly, my father's image. You will also see a colour photo, one of only ten colour photos, of a girl, the only girl: Me!! From an event to launch Ariel's new instamatic washing powder. I'm pretty sure the person to my left in the gallery won the Nobel Prize in Chemistry.

(From L to R): Aldous Huxley, HH Asquith, Graham Greene, Me, Cyril Norman Hinshelwood

Conjure up an image of an Oxford student. You'll be forgiven if the hapless soul you have envisioned in your mind's eye is a pale and pimply chap with glasses as thick as double-glazed windows, stumbling about nose-deep in a book. I was under the same impression when I applied to Balliol, hoping to continue what had become a bit of a family tradition—my father and grandfather both having read there.

Balliol College: home away from home, 1996–99

When I told Abba I was going to try to get into Oxford on the basis of academic merit he was nonplussed. I would have to apply to St Hilda's, he told me, the all-women's college founded in 1893 for those of the weaker sex who dared to think big. I had to break it to him gently that women had been allowed to study at Balliol since 1979. Luckily, by the time I was applying the rules had changed somewhat and you didn't have to sit the dreaded one-word entrance exam, described as the hardest in the world. Applicants were required to write a 3000-word essay on a single word—for instance, 'What is evil?' or 'What is patience?' There is a legendary story of the year when it was 'What is courage?' when one student famously wrote 'This is' and left the rest of the paper blank. No one seems to know what became of said student so it could very possibly be an urban myth or more likely that the professor failed him with the accompanying comment, 'No, this is stupidity.'

I was not so brave. When Mrs Prabhu, the principal of the British School where I had been a student for twelve years, called me to her office early one morning in the summer of 1996, I knew the A-level results were out and my fate had been decided. The offer from Balliol was two A's and a B, not an impossible ask, but my mock exams earlier that year had been a bit of a disaster—an A in history, as predicted, a B in economics and a Dreadful D in literature!

Mrs Narula, my literature teacher, told me my answers lacked empathy and feeling and I should do more theatre to help me relate better. That is how I landed the star role of Blanche du Bois in the twelfth standard's rendition of Tennessee Williams' play *A Streetcar Named Desire*. It was my shining moment—my whole family was coming to see me perform, including my father who had set foot in school a grand total of one time before this—to play a parent–child cricket match in which he scored 250 not out against a bunch of eleven-year-olds and nobody spoke to me for a week.

Before the play there was a small ten-minute skit where we were enacting a scene from *The Merchant of Venice*. My father thought that was it—my star moment as 'one of Portia's servants'—and left after the skit, before the main play had even begun!

'So what will it be?' Mrs Prabhu's expression was inscrutable as she handed me an envelope that seemed bizarrely thin given the weight of its contents. I opened it slowly, postponing the finality of a result, holding on to the comforting embrace of ambiguity. I forced

All good actors do theatre

myself to focus on the letters swimming drunkenly before my restless eyes. I had got three A's. I tried to understand my feelings. There was jubilation, of course. I had topped the class. My parents would be so proud. But there was also a nagging queasiness in the pit of my stomach. I would be going away to university. I would be going away from my home, my family, my country for the first time. And I would no longer be the smartest girl in the class; I would be a small fish in a very very big pond—a pond where all the fish wore thick glasses and quoted Descartes and made jokes like: Jean-Paul Sartre walks into a bar and says to the bartender, 'I'd like a cup of coffee please, with no cream.' The bartender replies, 'I'm so sorry but we're out of cream. How about with no milk?'

Eh.

We left Delhi for London a week before my eighteenth birthday. Abba, Amman and I. In 1952, when he got admission into the college, Abba's journey had taken two weeks by ship. The same 6000-odd kilometres took us a mere nine hours on a plane but I am sure I felt the same trepidation he had. The night before our departure I remember sitting on my bed, deciding whether or not to pack Jamun, my purple bunny, when Amman knocked on the door.

'Abba doesn't think it's a good idea but I want you to have this,' she said, placing a small red object in my hands. My first mobile phone.

Until then we had only had the one landline with an infinitely long extension cord which you could follow through corridors, across landings, until you reached the inevitable dead end that it was snaked under—Apa's locked door. And then you had to knock beseechingly for what seemed an eternity whilst she chattered on with Laila about who was cuter, Tom Cruise or Brad Pitt. Abba had a mobile phone but it was always switched off.

'I'll turn it on when I want to call someone,' he would say. 'It's to make other people available to me, not to make me available to other people.'

Mobile phones were also very expensive then, and the calls made from them exorbitant. The first commercial Motorola mobile phone offered thirty minutes of talk time, six hours standby, could store thirty numbers and cost close to 4000 USD (do the conversion to Indian rupees and you'll know just how expensive that was!). But that was way back in 1983.

In 1996 my Nokia 2110 cost close to Rs 50,000 and had only basic functions like calling and sending/receiving messages but it wasn't the expense my father objected to. It was the inverse snobbery he feared I would be subjected to at Balliol which was known to be more left-leaning in thought than the other colleges. Signs of unearned affluence were judged harshly there and my mother made me promise to keep this scarlet symbol of substance well hidden from censorious eyes.

And then, suddenly, the day was upon us. I remember them dropping me to my room, unloading my luggage, taking me to lunch and then saying goodbye. I didn't want them to go but I couldn't let them know how terrified I was. Abba was feeling nostalgic—he pointed out the drainpipe he and his friends would scale to sneak back into college once the gates were locked at midnight.

'Make sure you're back in time,' he told me.

'Abba, they give us a key now,' I told him gently.

I could tell he was having trouble processing the steely march of progress even in this little bastion of tradition. The quad was littered with families embracing their children—cheerful waves and slaps on the back. I refused to cry. When your life flashes before your eyes there are a few images that you know will make the cut and this was one of them: The navy blue rented sedan kicking up dust as it drove away, carrying my parents further and further away from me, and with them my childhood.

I forced myself to turn away from the receding car and walk towards the common room where freshers were already congregating—all of them seemed self-assured and effortlessly cool. There was a willowy girl with flaming red spikes for hair who was sitting on a trunk and regaling the others in a thick northern Irish accent. There was a pale boy with astonishingly blue eyes in a floor-length dark coat rolling a cigarette in the corner. Boisterous laughter emanated from a group of beefy boys in rugby shirts play wrestling by the window. Where were all the bespectacled geeks? I had been to one school my whole life and consequently I had forgotten how to make friends. How was I supposed to approach these people?

I will be forever grateful to one girl with a warm maternal vibe who understood my plight and came to my rescue. Let's call her Cathy, because that was her name. She thrust a mug of sugary tea at me to fortify the nerves and hustled me into a non-threatening circle of average-looking people exchanging notes on what subject they had enrolled for, where they were from, what school they had been to, etc. My conversation was desperate. I wanted to be liked. I wanted to be accepted. I didn't want to be friendless. But I soon realized that even though I was the only 'fresh-off-the-boat' Indian, we were all more or less in the same boat. A few of us arranged to meet up for dinner in the hall at 7 p.m. and I went off to settle into my room, hide my mobile phone, and work up an appetite for such an unreasonably early dinner.

It took me three whole months to settle in at Oxford. I was bitterly cold. Sure, Delhi winters could be harsh but our beds back home were pre-warmed with hot-water bottles every night and our bathwater heated in buckets to an ideal temperature. We all had dinner huddled together by a fire, sitting on mattresses around a low, square table with a quilt draped over it covering our legs, toasty from the *angithi* burning underneath. My room at Balliol on the other hand was built in the thirteenth century and had escaped even a hint of renovation since. There was a single bed, a desk and a chair, one slim cupboard, a basin with two faucets—one yielding numbingly cold water and the other scalding—and an electric heater. You had to climb on to the desk to peer out of the one window that overlooked the cheery vista of Martyrs' Memorial which commemorated three Protestants burnt at the stake in the sixteenth century for heresy. The electric heater was my best friend my first few weeks there. I would wear a sweater and two pairs of socks, wrap myself in my 16.5 tog duvet and basically hibernate, coming out only to forage for food (giant bars of Twix, pot noodle and Diet Coke). One night, in a feat that would put Icarus to shame, I fell asleep too close to the heater and managed to set my duvet on fire. Fortunately the ultra-sensitive fire alarm went off, causing me crushing embarrassment but saving my life. That was when I decided enough was enough. The heater could warm my fingers and toes, but I needed to make friends to melt the ice around my homesick heart.

Those of you who have studied away from home know that you spend the better part of your three years at university trying to get rid of the friends you made after that fourth gin and tonic at the freshers' week ABBA-themed party. No offence to Jack, Jill, Mary and Humpty Dumpty (not real names).

Luckily I soon met Charlotte and Tom (real names). Tom helped me expand my horizons, literally. In the spring breaks we travelled through Europe and Africa together, hitch-hiking from the Oxford city centre to the Eiffel Tower in Paris, backpacking through the quaint Spanish towns of Toledo and Granada, exploring the Sahara Desert atop camels we named Ixa and Humpy Thing, whilst reading 1001 Arabian Nights, feasting on tagines in Fez and oranges in Marrakesh and marvelling at how seedy and unromantic Casablanca really was.

Tom and I—the call of the trail

Charlotte lived across the corridor from me and we became friends while waiting in line to use the one bathroom all fourteen of us on Staircase XVII had to share. Someone was having a tub-bath and so we got chatting about India and how a diet of processed food and aerated drinks was severely constipating—in hindsight I think I was doing all the talking—when the bathroom door opened and a young man came out, towel around waist and soap in hand. I was about to enter when a girl came out after him, shaking the excess water from her hair. I tried to hide my amazement at this casual exhibition of communal bathing and made for the door again when, incredibly, another man came out whistling a merry tune. This time I couldn't help but stare slack-jawed at him, my cheeks red with embarrassment. To be honest, I felt like a prude for being so Victorian. It was quite responsible of them really, I tried to reason—think of all the water they must have saved by not bathing independently. I looked at Charlotte, then at the tub and then back at Charlotte.

'There are some showers across the quad,' she said, breaking the awkward silence, and we both fell into a fit of giggles. That very night I wrote to my mother asking her to send me a *balti* and a lota, post-haste. Unfortunately the concept of a bucket bath is alien to the British and my precious balti was consequently used for mopping purposes, as a makeshift stool and on the weekends for drunken students to indiscriminately throw up in.

Charlotte, Tom and I lived together in a house in our second year with four other people. In our fourth week there I confessed to them about the Nokia phone and waited for their expressions to turn disapproving. Thankfully my father's fears were unfounded and they looked, at worst, uninterested. Were it not for them I would have found it much harder to adjust. As it is, there was nothing regular about being a student at Oxford. We did not have regular classes—Oxbridge prides itself on its tutorial system, so once a week you research and write a 2000-word essay and then spend an hour discussing it with your tutor, one-on-one. It is considered an incredible opportunity to learn from the experts who have written most of the books on the subject of choice. You would think then that we would spend the better part of the week studying hard, putting our carefully weighed words on paper to glean the most from this amazing chance—but somehow, between costume parties (where I would rack my brain time and time again to think of some ingenious ensemble, and time and time again I would resort to my Ritu Kumar green salwar suit and go as 'some kind of Indian princess'), pub crawls, burning pasta and watching daytime TV, the week would slip away, and we would inevitably find ourselves pulling the dreaded all-nighter.

My tutorial was scheduled from 4 to 5 p.m. on a Thursday afternoon. At 4 p.m. on Wednesday was when I got down to my desk to speed-read the forty-odd essays and books on my reading list and then hastily scramble together my sleep-deprived notions. My tutorials were nerve-racking—not enough sleep, too much coffee, creases from my pillow lining my face and drool still caked to my cheek as I faced the man who had written the book that I had pretended to read and then copied liberally from. In short, a nightmare.

Then there was the age-old tradition of wearing a uniform called subfusc for exams—a black suit for boys and a black skirt, white shirt and black jacket for women, with a big billowing black robe and a black ribbon around the neck.

You must also carry a hat, called a mortar board, which you are never ever allowed to wear. And if that's not stressful enough, for your first exam you must wear a white carnation in your buttonhole, a pink one for the ensuing exams and a red carnation for your last exam.

As a result, the night before our final exams, instead of revising our notes in the library, we would be tearing our rooms apart in a state of blind panic looking for anything that could be fashioned into an improvised black ribbon! There is also the bizarre tradition of 'trashing' students coming out of their final exam with flour, eggs, champagne, baked beans—basically anything else left over in your fridge from last night's dinner! So when I exited the grand hall in the summer of 1999 hoping to finally feel the sun on my face after months of vitamin D–deprived dedication and to breathe in the invigorating air of liberation from academia, I was met instead with a mouthful of rotten eggs and doused in a gloopy cake mix from hell.

A common sight at university was the recently dumped boyfriend/girlfriend who had come to college as one half of a solid partnership that neither time nor distance could tear asunder. I watched each of these committed long-distance relationships crumble one by one until only one remained. Benjamin and Jennifer were our star couple. Jennifer studied at Bristol and we looked to them for hope when the world seemed too cruel to bear, and the radiance of their love never failed to soothe our troubled souls.

'All the disadvantages of being in a relationship, and none of the advantages,' it is said of long-distance romance. But Ben and Jen were unmoved by the cynics. Towards the beginning of the second year, when Jen left Benjamin for Dave, who could play the ukulele and was such a good listener, she didn't just break his heart; she shattered our collective belief that love could survive long-distance. We took turns to sit with Ben under the oak tree, cursing Douchebag Dave who had stolen our Jen, and swigging from bottles of liquid anaesthetic.

So what was the sum of my Oxford education? A yellowing parchment securing a BA Honours in modern history from the premier educational institution in the world—sure there's that, but it was so much more than that. I learnt how to catch a bus, how to use a washing machine, how many gin and tonics I could drink with my judgement intact (2.5), how to manage a bank account and live on a budget, how to play pool, how to say no to drugs and not feel uncool, how to be an ambassador for my country in a foreign land, how I like my eggs cooked, never to wax my eyebrows . . . and that when you strip away all cultural affectations, you can make a genuine and lasting connection with people if you can accept, embrace and simply be who you are. But first you have to find yourself. And sometimes you need to travel 6000 kilometres to do that.

Time is a slippery mistress. Feel free to reimagine that sentence with a more elegant metaphor. Just when I was starting to feel at home, when I had forged real bonds with people, when I finally understood what Professor Conway wanted from my essays, it was time to up and leave. It was time to face the outside world. It was so difficult to accept that we were all never going to be in that one place again. There would be reunions, of course, but it wouldn't be the same. Our graduation ceremony was a sombre affair. Students wore the subfusc and this time, as graduates, we were finally allowed to wear our mortar boards. There was some last-moment panic

Does this mean I need to get a job now?

when I looked down and saw that my feet in my new black heels were missing the mandatory black stockings women must wear. It was too late to go to the shops and I was furious with myself for forgetting. I wasn't going to be able to graduate because of a pair of absent socks. And then my father came to my rescue—he took off his shoes, took off his socks and handed them over to me.

They were four sizes too big but they were black and that was all that mattered. I may never know what it feels like to walk in my father's shoes, a mantle my brother has inherited, but I can say that I once walked in his socks. And those 100 metres were the most defining of my life.

The ceremony itself was not how I had imagined it would be. I had expected speeches, a live band, cheering crowds and confetti. Instead everyone was seated silently in a predefined order in the grand old Sheldonian Theatre.

The grand old Sheldonian

A very very old lady read out some Latin for an hour, there was a sceptre and a lot of nodding and quite frankly I didn't understand a word of it. No one really does unless you're ancient Roman. I had almost nodded off when my neighbour nudged me in the ribs, indicating it was my turn to go up to collect my degree. As I bent down on one knee in front of the vice chancellor, I couldn't resist glancing

at my parents. The look on their faces made me feel . . . well . . . pretty darn awesome. I don't think Abba had ever been so proud. There are many good

A proud papa

universities to graduate from in the world, but at the end of the day there's only one worth taking your socks off for.

Hurrah! Class of 1999

5

Wakeful City

It was all going so well. It was 2002, I was twenty-three years old, I had a plan and I was on track. I was working at Citigroup Private Bank in Mumbai as a Management Associate, a post-MBA designation with a coveted salary and a number of valued perks, the most prized being the assured transfer to London within eighteen months of commencement. My job description read 'High Net Worth Asset Management'. In other words how to get rich by making rich people richer. An indisputably sensible career choice for the young and ambitious, and one I knew my parents approved of. They had invested substantially in my first-rate education and soon the returns on that investment would start to show.

Human Resources was stymied by my presence at Citibank. Every time I had to go to the department to get my expenses vetted or to collect the latest banking compliance guidelines I would be greeted by staff members unable to contain their curiosity. 'Why are you working here?' 'Don't you want to be an actress?' 'Do you need this job?' I don't think it was their intention to make me feel unwelcome but sometimes I felt like my desire to earn my own money was a frivolous whim that was depriving someone genuinely in need of employment. I would hastily finish my work with them, turn tail and run back to the sanctuary of the small cabin I shared with my boss. There was not a lot of time for introspection: The work was unfamiliar and intense and my days were long and tiring. I would make the commute every day from my 2BHK rental at Rs 17,000 a month in Lokhandwala to Lower Parel at first and later, when the head office moved, to Bandra Kurla Complex. By the time I got home from work there was only enough time to shower, microwave my pre-cooked dinner, swat mosquitoes for an hour and then fall asleep watching TV.

Investment banking is a great turn-on for many people but it did nothing for my mojo. Frankly, forget loving the job, I barely understood it—calculating the yield to maturity of a bond or comparing the internal rates of return of investments was simply beyond me. I sat through countless meetings with clients, selling them highly sophisticated and personally tailored investment products, knowing full well that if their questions were to scratch at the meticulously manicured membrane of mumbo jumbo, I would be exposed. Even today, when my private bankers come home to analyse my portfolio, they speak to me as a former banker accustomed to their industry acronyms. When they refer to the need for ABS I nod wisely and my hand involuntarily moves towards my midsection before I realize they mean Asset-Backed Securities. I have to keep reminding myself SLB is Securities Lending and Borrowing, not Sanjay Leela Bhansali and to them PC is P. Chidambaram, not Priyanka Chopra! I make non-committal noises at their suggestions and leave the room under some pretext only to call up my second-opinion financial adviser for her reaction, which I then return to the room and confidently regurgitate.

The job then was a means to an end—a secure life in England, the country I had spent the last half-decade in and was starting to call home. Not everyone has a dream job. Not everyone knows exactly what they want to be from when they are six years old. When I was six I wanted to do manual labour. I spent the afternoons camped out in the garden, sweeping dead leaves off the veranda and eating orange biscuits and water for food.

At the age of nine I discovered money and I couldn't get enough of it. I became an entrepreneur. First I sold cosmetics to the staff, ideal customers who couldn't say no to me. I gathered up all the used make-up my mother had tossed into the bin—almost empty bottles of nail polish and lipstick, near bare pots of cold cream—placed them

Being enterprising with my
photography chops

on a tray and marched down to the servants' quarters. Each item was then 'sold' to my captive consumers for a grand sum of Rs 2. Inevitably there was rioting in the ranks and news of my greedy exploits reached my mother's horrified ears. My flourishing business was forced into immediate closure and I got my first lesson in economic protectionism versus a free market. So I branched out—I packed a small suitcase with a plastic syringe, some small towels, a box of Band-Aids and a fistful of mints and went around the house administering medical aid to those I thought in need. Headaches were treated with a cold compress and a mint in lieu of aspirin, joint and muscle pains eased with massages, and injections were given for more baffling ailments. The fee for each visit was again the grand sum of Rs 2. My doctor's practice was actually quite successful and received much encouragement from all members of the household; I was even offered the handsome sum of Rs 25 from an anonymous investor to buy balms and ointments when I turned ten and outgrew the business.

When I was twelve I was reading the Famous Five and Nancy Drew books and so, naturally, the only possible career option in my mind was that of a detective. My father didn't take well to my following him around the house, jotting down notes on who he was seeing and what he was doing, and that was soon the end of that vocation. The following week I was enrolled in the Delhi School of Music, first for ballet classes—I was unceremoniously dropped from these within the month with the forthright explanation that I had the grace of a five-legged spider—and then for piano lessons in which I fared only marginally better. My family was then subjected to endless post-dinner recitals of 'Twinkle Twinkle Little Star' and 'London Bridge is Falling Down' for which the admission fee was—you guessed it— Rs 2 per person!

Virtually a virtuoso

Twelve years later, at twenty-four, sitting in my corporate cabin overlooking the business hub of BKC, I would ask myself if I had made the right career choice and if there was such a thing as the *right* career choice. I wanted to be financially independent, free to make my own decisions. I wanted to earn enough to lead the lifestyle to which I had grown accustomed, which included air conditioning, travel, a diet rich in overpriced exotic fruit and adding to my most cherished possession: my ever-expanding library of books.

Banking made all that and more possible and then there was the lure of London. But I had felt instinctively on moving to Mumbai and taking up the job at Citibank that this was not what I wanted to do with my life. I had even called up Amman to say that I wasn't happy and that I wanted to return to Delhi.

'Give it three months,' she told me. 'You have never enjoyed change, and you need time to adjust so give it three months and if you're still unhappy then come home.'

This was what being an adult was all about, I told myself. Not doing the fun thing or the easy thing or the impulsive thing but doing the right thing and sticking it out.

To ease the transition phase Amman gave me the number of her friend's son who had also moved from Delhi to work in Mumbai and was obviously enjoying it more than I was.

'You need to make friends and Rohan is a lovely boy. I have never met him but he must be. His father went to Harvard.'

I figured there was no harm in testing this feeble theory and called Rohan that night. We arranged to meet the following Friday to see a play at Prithvi followed by dinner at the Marriott. What followed was one of my two most embarrassing text message-related stories. (The other I cannot tell you as I am sworn to secrecy but let me just say it involved the words 'I love you chickadpoo' and was meant to be sent on behalf of a young relative of mine to her father but went instead to the head of a major pharmaceutical corporation whose name starts with Bhai . . .)

After the play ended, we made our way to the Italian restaurant Mezzo Mezzo at the Marriott. I excused myself and went to the loo, leaving Rohan to order drinks.

'Bored witless and we haven't even eaten yet. Yawn.'—I typed the message out to send to my best friend Priyanka, but before I could stop myself I had sent it to Rohan instead.

To Rohan. Rohan who was sitting outside waiting for me. I almost dropped the phone in horror as my heart started to pound in my chest. I was rooted to the floor. Well, there was no option: I was not going out there, I would just stay in the bathroom cubicle all night.

After about ten minutes I decided I had to face the music and stepped out hoping he had left the restaurant in disgust. But no, there he was at the table reading the menu. He didn't look offended or upset in the least.

I sat down across from him and something compelled me to ask, 'Could I borrow your phone?'

He reached into his jacket pocket took out his mobile and stopped to switch it on before handing it over to me. He had turned it off during the play! I quickly opened the message inbox, found the new message from me and deleted it—all cool as a cucumber, might I add. Although I was grateful to the restaurant's dim lighting because I'm sure my face was as red as a lobster!

There must have been a cricket or tennis match going on somewhere because Rohan asked me, 'Are you checking the score?', a little puzzled as I continued to punch furiously at his phone. I can't actually remember what I said or how I explained myself to him—the crisis had been averted and I could breathe again. Rohan and I went on to become good friends and we remain so even today, although that may change if he happens to read this book.

Discomfited by variation but quick to adjust, the months passed without further incident and I fell into a routine. I made three friends at work—Soma, Kyle and Ashwin—who thankfully didn't judge me or treat me any differently because of who I was. I stopped flying home to Delhi every other weekend and started to explore Mumbai.

We are all familiar with the abiding battle over the age-old question of which is a better city to live in: Delhi or Mumbai? Wives have left husbands over this issue; families have been torn asunder. I was actually born in Mumbai, or Bombay as it was called then, but we moved to Delhi when I was four to live with Badi Amman when her health started to deteriorate. Having spent fifteen years in Delhi and an equal number of years (from 2002 to the present) in Mumbai, I think I am well positioned to offer some insights on the debate.

Delhi is the political capital, bursting with history, culture, lush green gardens and beautiful heritage monuments. The seasons actually change in Delhi and you can enjoy a proper winter complete with a luxurious wardrobe of coats, shawls and lined boots.

Unfortunately, to appreciate this you need to breathe in smog-filled air equivalent to smoking fourteen cigarettes a day and vogmasks have become a must-have style accessory.

Mumbai has seasons too: summer followed by the monsoon followed by—wait for it—a second summer. October is the hottest month of the year

Who wore it better?

here but even though the heat is clement compared to a scorching Delhi summer, the humidity dampens a newly coiffed hairdo as much as it does the effervescent human spirit. As for cultural colouring, all hail Prithvi Theatre, the National Centre for the Performing Arts and Jehangir Art Gallery which stand as glittering oases in an otherwise largely unedifying wasteland.

Having said all this, as a single working woman in India, which I was until very recently, Mumbai is the city to be in. It has been said of Mumbai that it is the city of dreams and dreamers—people come here to make something of their lives and even though many fail, few starve; the city welcomes hard workers and rewards them with opportunity. It is also universally hailed as a safer place to live in. Big egos and spoilt sons with presumably poor memories (Why else do they repeatedly feel compelled to ask if you know who their father is? 'Tu jaanta hai mera baap kaun hai?') own the streets of Delhi, instilling in others a sense of fear and insecurity. You think twice before taking on someone lacking in good manners or driving etiquette in the very real fear of a violent reprisal.

In Mumbai bumper-to-bumper traffic jams are a daily inconvenience but miraculously discipline still prevails. People stay in the correct lanes and wait patiently at zebra crossings. Once, I even saw a dog standing at a traffic signal cooling its heels until the lights turned red!

Ironically, the only time I have been a victim of crime has been in Mumbai when my flat was broken into by a thief in the dead of night. It was a beautiful bachelorette pad on the first floor of a very tastefully designed building and it was love at first sight. It was also the first flat I had seen. Common practice entails that you don't buy the very first property you see. At least that is what I was given to understand when I left school to go to university in England. My boyfriend at the time was going to study in the States and I had assumed we would attempt to survive the distance, at least for a while, but he was a very practical boy. He wrote me a letter which read: 'Relationships are like buying a house; you don't buy the first one you see. You shop around a bit to see what else is available. And yes, you may realize that the first one was the best and by that time it may be off the market, but that's a reasonable risk to take.' It took me a while to comprehend that I was being dumped for the plentiful fish in the sea across the seas. The metaphor was lost on me at the time, but years later, in 2008, when I was looking to buy my first house, his words came back to me, and they rang as hollow then as they had in 1996.

When you see something, or someone, special—and it's a rare and beautiful thing—don't take it for granted. Grab it and hold on tight. That's what I did.

First-floor flats are often avoided by single women because of the security implications of being so close to the road and therefore accessible to intruders. The typical first line of defence against this is the unsightly window grill, a common eyesore in the city. I was dead set against installing grills on my windows and the French doors that led to the bedroom balcony. I enjoyed an unfettered view of a rare tree-lined road outside and I felt completely safe in swanky suburban Bandra with buildings and people all around me. I lived happily grill-free and without incident for four whole years until one night in 2011.

It was December and I had gone to a party in South Mumbai, returning home at 2.30 a.m. Kunal had been away in Goa on a five-week outdoor, shooting for *Go Goa Gone* and this was his first night back. He had gone to a film screening in Bandra which ended late and so he decided to spend the night at my flat instead of driving back to his place in Versova. We chatted for a while and finally decided to turn in at 3.30 a.m.

That is why, at close to 4 a.m., when we heard a noise we were both instantly awake (although Kunal's version of the story is that I was fast asleep until he shook me awake, but as this is my book we'll go with my version). When you live in an apartment it is not unusual to hear thumps and bumps through the night and so I was not worried at first. Then I heard a soft thud from the balcony outside. I looked to Kunal for confirmation but he had already gotten out of bed and was crouching by the French windows, peering through the glass. Now, my mother, who wanted to create the illusion of a garden for me, had filled the balcony with a variety of differently sized plants, making it impossible for Kunal to distinguish felon from foliage.

I was about to ask him if he could see someone when he suddenly leapt up, yanked the curtain aside and revealed a lanky man, face covered with a handkerchief who had pried open the lock and had one foot in the door already! Kunal had the element of surprise which he used to his full advantage, kicking the intruder back on to the balcony. Kunal's right arm was in a cast at the time because he had torn some ligaments in an accident a few weeks prior to this and so he only had the use of his left hand.

I jumped out of bed, wringing both my good hands together in a singularly unhelpful fashion, for which I will never forgive myself. I couldn't see what was happening on the balcony but I heard them scuffling for a few seconds and then there was a shout and a thud. Kunal reappeared on the threshold with a haunted look in his eyes saying, 'I think he's dead.' The man had tried to escape, half-jumping half-falling from the balcony. Kunal says he saw it as if in slow motion—the man falling backwards, eyes staring up in alarm, and the crack of what we later discovered was his back breaking followed by silence.

We rushed down, stopping to wake the security guard (he had, of course, slept through all of this) who unlocked the main gate to the road where the man lay. Thankfully, he stirred. That was all I wanted to see, and once I knew he was alive I went back inside. I didn't want to see his face and be haunted by it in my dreams, or maybe I didn't want him to see mine. I called 100 for the first and only time in my life. The police van came within ten minutes and took him, Kunal and the security guard to the station to file charges and to get the man medical aid. It was only when I was back in my flat that the magnitude of what had happened, and what could have happened had Kunal not been there, as he had not been every night for the past five weeks, hit me.

When Kunal returned at 7 a.m. he told me the police had showed him the 'most-wanted' list on the noticeboard and pointed out our intruder's name at number two. They had even slapped him on the back and thanked him for doing their job but I could tell he was more than a little spooked by the fact that he had fought and nabbed a hardened criminal.

All in all it was the best possible outcome to the situation—nobody was hurt (except the neighbourhood thief who had a hairline fracture), nothing had been stolen, the thief had been apprehended and Kunal had proved himself a real-life hero in the fight or flight response test. Needless to say the following day window grills with sturdy locks were installed throughout the house. You never think it's going to happen to you until it does. I continue to feel safe in Mumbai in a way that I don't in Delhi but I don't feel invincible any more—at home and on the streets; I am a little bit more wary of things that go bump in the night.

If Mumbai is the city that has given me my only run-in with crime, it is also the city that came to my rescue in 2005 when thousands of people were killed and the city came to a three-day standstill because of the floods. Torrential rain lashed Maharashtra on 26 July—it was the eighth ever twenty-four-hour recorded rainfall figure of 944 mm.

Like many others that day I found myself stranded, after my car stalled on S.V. Road, 8 kilometres from home (Lokhandwala at the time). I couldn't get through to anyone, I didn't know how to get home and it was pouring relentlessly. I abandoned my car with a note taped to the inside of the windscreen saying I would be back to pick it up the following day and tried to follow the spontaneous human chain that had formed in the middle of the road but my flimsy chappals made it difficult to get a firm footing. The water was rising and had reached my waist and I could feel the insistent pull of an invisible current tugging at me. The side roads looked like small rivers leading off to a dark, watery grave; the odd animal carcass floated by every now and then. It was a bizarre and grotesque scene. I should have been terrified but what I remember is how warm and friendly complete strangers were to me, stopping in their tracks to direct me, offer me drinking water and the use of their phones.

I finally managed to get through to my mother in Delhi who called my colleague in Khar (for some reason I couldn't get through to anyone in the city) and asked him to find me while I sat shivering on a stationary BEST bus (I confess that that is the only time I have sat on a public bus), my sole refuge from the punishing rain. I remember being acutely conscious of my bedraggled appearance—I was sopping wet, hair plastered to my head, mascara streaking my face—and hoping fervently that I was unrecognizable to the others on the bus.

Two women sitting across the aisle glanced at me a few times and whispered to each other. I considered getting off the bus and melting away into the nameless crowd but the absurdity of being vain in this situation hit me. I turned to face them, inviting them to see me, the real me, not an actor or a face on a billboard, but just a girl stranded in the rain, much like themselves.

'It has to stop sometime, don't worry,' the one closer to me said and the simple logic of that was immensely comforting. I realized that they were not judging me; it was I who was judging them. Having been perennially sized up and ogled at during my years in Delhi, I feared a gigantic metropolis like Mumbai with its teeming crowds would eat me alive, and there I was, totally defenceless, without even a basic protective layer of make-up! I couldn't have been more wrong. I ended up chatting away amiably with the two women—we knew it would not be an enduring friendship but for those two hours we were comfortable companions of circumstance.

I will be forever grateful to Shawn, my colleague, for leaving the safety and security of his house to scour all the stalled buses on S.V. Road in search of me, someone he really didn't know all that well. When he finally found me, we sought shelter in Santa Cruz at the home of his friend who gave me a change of clothes and a hot meal. At daybreak I decided to continue the journey home on foot.

The streets were full of people serving tea, biscuits, water and bananas to those who had been marooned through the night. In all it took me twenty-three hours to get back to my flat, but that day, as I trudged through waterlogged lanes, I felt a bond form with the city and its people, their resilience and compassion. I felt proud to have chosen to settle down here, to call Mumbai my

On the sets of *Tum Mile*—bringing back a flood of memories

home. I think it was this experience that made me so keen to do *Tum Mile*, the 2009 love story film set against the backdrop of this very deluge.

Why else would one choose to spend forty days in stagnant waist-deep water, under powerful ceiling rain machines on a 100x250-feet studio floor in Bhandup, one of the oldest suburbs in Mumbai—hardly the most glamorous of settings!

Our director Kunal Deshmukh actually wore a scuba-diving suit to work each day and at one point I heard him announce on the mic, *'Yahan pe koi thukega nahin, koi pishaab nahin karega!'* 'Nobody will spit in the water, nobody will urinate here.' 'Yahan' being the water we were all working in. He was looking pointedly at a light man who had not taken a bathroom break in eight hours, when the rest of us had taken at least two each!

Did someone say there's soup?

How I feel without coffee? Depresso.

The flooding may have proved that Delhi has better social and economic facilities than Mumbai, but what it lacks in infrastructure Mumbai more than makes up for with civilization. My faith in this city has been reaffirmed time and time again—be it during the suburban train blasts of July 2006 or the terror attacks of November 2008. The city refuses to be brought to its knees. Call it an undying spirit or just plain necessity, even the hardened cynic would have to accept that there exists a humanity here that prompts people to rescue strangers, makes crowds throng to blood donation camps and helping hands to disaster relief.

I was about to book my ticket back to Delhi when Amman told me to give Mumbai three months. That was fifteen years ago. Since then I have put down roots here—this is my place of residence, my place of work, where I met and married my husband. I may have spent my growing-up years in Delhi but I grew up in Mumbai—this is where I finally found the courage to radically overhaul my carefully constructed career plan, to turn my back on life in London, to forsake my cushy corporate job and with it the approval of my parents, to embark on a shaky career in the very industry I had assiduously steered clear of. This is where I entered Bollywood.

6

A Working Actor

I had a friend in school who could make a map of the world from memory in under ten minutes. I thought it was a skill worth learning—especially useful for when you pick the Person/Place/Animal category in Pictionary—but, when I looked at references to copy from, I found that every map was different. The most common map, the one hanging in your school's geography classroom for instance, is the Mercator projection map drawn way back in 1596 to help sailors navigate the world. It has all the land masses with their particular shapes—the horn of Africa, boot-shaped Italy—but the sizes are all wrong.

North America is made to look as vast as Africa, the Scandinavian countries bigger than India, and China smaller than Greenland. In reality, India is three times the size of all the Scandinavian countries put together, China is four times larger than Greenland and you could fit three North Americas into Africa.

So why did this happen?

Gerardus Mercator, the map-maker, was German and when deciding where to centre his projection of the earth, he arbitrarily chose his own country, Germany. As a result the equator was placed not halfway down as it should be but two-thirds of the way down and sizes were distorted in favour of the wealthier lands of the north.

Unlike other great scholars of the age, Mercator opted not to travel and acquired his knowledge of geography from a vast library of books and interactions with visiting travellers, merchants and statesmen instead. Had he ventured out more, perhaps his work would have been a more accurate reflection of fact.

But it's not just his map, any flat map of the earth is a lie because the earth itself is not flat. You simply cannot show the entire surface of a spherical-ish earth on a flat surface. The centre of this representation of the earth then becomes an ideological one guided by national pride, as in the case of Mercator, or religious persuasion with some Muslims choosing Mecca to be the centre of their world and some Christians, Jerusalem.

So the only map you can trust is a globe, and even a cursory glance at one will reveal a deep truth—there is no surface centre of the earth, only an inner core 6000-kilometres deep, a solid sphere made of iron with a temperature close to that of the surface of the sun. By now you must be wondering why I am subjecting you to an obtuse lesson in cartography so I'll stop circumambulating the globe and get to the point.

If Mercator, hailed for his erudition as the foremost mathematician of his time, thought Germany acceptable as the fulcrum around which the world revolves, then the quintessential Hindi movie actor can be easily forgiven for thinking that Bollywood is the centre of the world and that the only lives worth noting are those of the stars who fill the print, electronic and online media. In fact most people—even the non-celestial—tend to live life merely on the surface. They get caught up in the daily grind of work, chores and bills, and before they know it their lives, or at least the part that's worth living, is over.

Actors are especially susceptible to this shallowness. Intent on their individual life maps, they see the world with themselves at the centre—every success exaggerated, every failure amplified.

My first on-screen appearance was a very respectable one. The Hindi film *Dooriyan* (1979), starring Sharmila Tagore and Uttam Kumar, deals with marital discord—where the personal ambitions of an urban working couple and the responsibilities of marriage, namely raising a child, create seemingly irreconcilable differences between them. There is a song where my mother is holding their child, a mere infant, in her arms and trying to get it to sleep. That infant was me.

On-screen mothers

The film received huge acclaim as a rare progressive vision of modern urban relationships. And what I lacked in dialogue and clothing, I more than made up for in gravitas and believability. Thirty-odd years later I would rock my own borrowed baby to sleep in *31st October*. Apart from that similarity of action, performed by every leading lady at some point in her line of work, there has been little that my career has had in common with my mother's.

Amman is a superstar, a living legend, Bollywood royalty. I am what is called a 'working actor'—this essentially means I am an actor who while I may never achieve superstardom, have had a long and productive career, earn a better than decent living and have the admiration of my peers (to the extent that anyone today has the admiration of their peers!). My achievements are assuredly meritorious and allow me to hold my head high in society, but I am aware that when compared to Amman's, they pale like a gluten-free muffin in the face of red velvet.

You would not be wrong to wonder then why an academically inclined, stability-seeking private banker chose to jettison her corporate job with its cushy perks for the mercurial medium of the movies, and with it, the inevitably unfavourable comparisons to iconic mothers and brothers. I will get to the why, but first let me tell you the how.

So there I was pushing papers at Citibank in 2003—less than content but not unhappy and certainly not motivated enough to actually do anything about it—when I received a phone call that would change my life. Amol Palekar called me and asked if we could meet to discuss a film he was directing. I could have just said I wasn't interested in acting in movies or I already had a job and a plan or that my parents would be furious I was even considering this. Instead I said, 'How's Saturday?' and then went home to speed-watch every Amol Palekar film my DVD guy could source. There is no harm in meeting him, I thought. Surely it would be disrespectful to refuse such a senior member of the industry, I told myself. Also there was no need to share this development with anyone who may read more into my inconsistent disposition.

I didn't need to remind myself that acting in Hindi movies was a career option I had summarily dismissed at the age of eighteen when a very well-established director came to our home in Delhi to meet my mother, offering me a starring role opposite a properly famous hero. The idea of dropping out of Oxford to act in a Hindi film was so alien to me it was laughable and, much to the relief of my secretly terrified parents, I rolled my eyes at the proposal and never gave it or the few other offers that came my way a second thought.

Hindi movies were simply ludicrous: loud and unrealistic, filled with regressive characters spontaneously breaking into song and choreographed dance at the drop of a dupatta. Or so I thought. In my defence, it was the 1990s, not exactly the golden age of Indian cinema— made infamous by dialogues such as this gem: *'Mera naam hai Pote, jo apne baap ke bhi nahin hote,'* or *'Tune meri behen ko maar daala, theek kiya. Magar tune meri behen ka rape kiya, bahut bura kiya.'* You can't make this stuff up!

Thankfully, when we met at his office, the story Amol Palekar narrated to me was a very different one. His film was based on a Rajasthani folk tale and was about a young wife, Lachchi, whose husband leaves her the day after their wedding to go on a five-year business trip. The wife is then visited by a ghost, disguised as her husband, who is in love with her and takes her husband's place. The ghost is warm and winsome and much more attractive in demeanour to both Lachchi and to the family than the real husband, Kishanlal.

When Kishanlal returns at the end of five years, Lachchi is presented a riddle between the manifestation of all of her desires in the form of the ghost and her real husband. At the time Amol ji wanted to call the film Ghost Ka Dost and he wanted me to play the role of Lachchi. I immediately fell in love with the script and all its fantastical magic. I imagined myself as the vivacious Lachchi and when presented with my own riddle of Citibank versus Cinema I chose the charm and allure of Cinema.

The truth of the matter is that, given the opportunity, everyone wants to be a hero and, much to my chagrin, I too was not above this flight of fancy. The role of Kishanlal was to be played by a new actor; the film would introduce us both and I was told we needed to do a couple of months of workshopping, followed by three months of shooting in Rajasthan.

I was aware that to do this film, even as a one-off, I would have to quit my job at the bank. I had faced the camera before; I don't mean *Dooriyan*, but a more substantial role (four seconds long) when my father, among other sporting legends, was asked to carry a torch

It's not a low resolution photograph—we're just too fast for the camera!

of national integration on a short programme called *Spread the Light of Freedom*. This was way back in 1988 when there was only one TV channel in India, Doordarshan (those of you of that vintage will remember the green genie from *Alif Laila* and India's most loved superhero Shaktimaan). You can find a list of the prominent sports stars who ran with the torch: P.T. Usha, Kapil Dev, Milkha Singh, Sunil Gavaskar, Prakash Padukone, M.A.K. Pataudi—and Soha Ali Khan (thrown in last-minute for her irresistible cuteness, aged ten). The more cynical among you may remain unconvinced by these cinematic credentials and I grudgingly accept that my parents may possibly have had some hand in my being cast in *Dooriyan* and *Spread the Light*, but the Samsung ad I was to do many years later was all me!

It was halfway through my stint at Citibank that I was cast as director Homi Adajania's girlfriend in an advertisement for a Samsung television which claimed to emit bio-rays that relaxed not just your eyes but your whole body. It begins with a couple sitting on the couch, arguing. The girl turns away from the boy in anger and, at a loss for the right placatory words, the boy turns on the TV. Soothing rays in the form of rose petals radiate from the television set and envelop the

TV makes you happy

couple in a mist of tranquillity, dissipating the tension and enabling their happy reconciliation. Do look it up on YouTube—as of writing this book it has 1439 views and it could do with some more.

Being cast in a glossy advertisement is either the successful result of hard work and dedication in the form of diet, exercise, investment in an expensive photo shoot for some glamorous headshots, and exhaustive auditions—or the culmination of a random but fortuitous series of circumstances, also known as 'being in the right place at the right time'.

For me it was the latter. The right place being on the sofa in the study in my brother's house and the right time being when the ad film-maker, who happened to be a friend of Bhai's, came home for dinner. I'd like to think he saw me and was captivated by my fresh, dewy appeal and the sincerity of my television-watching face ... and who is to say he wasn't? The point being that as I contemplated leaving Citibank to embark on an artistic adventure with Amol Palekar as the new captain of my ship, I could truthfully state that I had persuasive prior experience in film, television and advertising. And given the somewhat indispensable involvement of Amman in film, Abba in TV and Bhai in advertising, I was keen to take this step into the abyss by myself.

The more discerning cinephiles among you may have recognized the Amol Palekar film as *Paheli* (2005) which, incidentally, was also India's official entry to the Oscars that year. You will have also remembered that the role of the lively and lovable Lachchi was played not by yours truly but by Rani Mukherjee. And the role of Kishanlal was not played by a debutant actor but the complete opposite of that—Shah Rukh Khan.

And therein lies the irony which laces life like one of Alanis Morissette's bitter pills. The film that finally made me quit my stable and secure job for a life of uncertainty, risk and insecurity, didn't happen—or, more accurately, it didn't happen for me.

I had just about convinced Human Resources of my commitment to the job and total lack of interest in becoming an actress when I decided I was, in fact, very interested in acting in a film and had no sense of commitment to the job. I handed in my notice and walked out of the bank, braving the accusatory stares of colleagues; their eyes

Bombay 1978, a star is born (literally, as 'Soha' means star in Arabic)

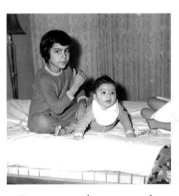

Does anyone know a good
eyebrow threader?

Okay, so we've established that I was born
in a pre–colour photography era

At the zoo—I much preferred the brass elephant at the entrance
to the real ones stuck inside

My dress is made from leftover upholstery from the sofa

Abba leading the team before a Winchester College football match at school (Winchester, Eton and Harrow did not play rugby but had their own ancient ball games)

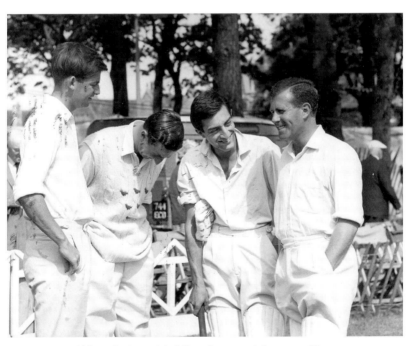

Abba relaxing with fellow Sussex cricketers at Hove

My favourite picture of my parents—from their wedding celebrations

Always and forever, engagement, 1966

Turf club reception with Raj Kapoor

Turf club reception with Asha Parekh and her mother

Branches of a family tree

Amman's seventieth birthday at Sher Bagh, Ranthambore National Park

Lost in the crowd—Summer 2015, London

Going Dutch—Summer 2015, Amsterdam

Summer 2014, Maldives

Chasing the sun

Big brothers are always in your corner

Words of advice before tying the knot

Mehendi moment

Eternal vows are a solemn affair

Swept off my feet

Sibling revelry

Are we really doing this?

Meet the Royals

Family portrait

Finally one where we all have our eyes open (from Bhai and
Kareena's wedding)

Does it get any better than this?

Can you spot the baby?

Amman is thinking, My hair used to
be that colour once

The calm before the storm

shouted 'hypocrite' at me but I didn't care because I was finally free of boring bonds and dull debentures.

The very next day Amol ji called me to say that they had decided to go in a different direction with the film. It may not have been the very next day but in my recollection of events it seemed to follow directly, like guilt after a chocolate binge. It was a direction, he said, that involved superstars and a bigger production and marketing budget, and that regrettably left no room for me. And so there I was: sans job, sans salary, sans having told my parents about loss of said job and salary, and very much sans a plan.

And that is how my first film, my 'big' debut, came to be a small Bengali film, *Iti Srikanta* (2004), in which I played an ashram-confined Vaishnavite called Kamalata who rarely spoke (thankfully, as I am far from fluent in Bangla). The producers met me in Mumbai—they

First frame

explained it was a small-budget film and so they could pay me a very minimal amount. Let's just say my laundry bill for the month was more than my fee. We would be shooting in Santiniketan for four weeks and so would stay in a guest house, there being no hotels in the vicinity. It was not exactly the glamorous launch I had imagined but the film was a period drama based on Sarat Chandra's 1917 novel *Srikanta* and it was going to be directed by two-time National Award–winning director Anjan Das. I decided it was the ideal test of my wanting to be an actor—in rural Bengal, away from the media glare, I could discover for myself whether I enjoyed the process of film-making, of being in front of the camera and playing a part. And if I didn't I could quietly resume my earlier life in a more corporate setting.

I will always remember the first time I faced the camera—except I wasn't really facing it; it was off to the side but still so close I could reach out and touch it. Adil Hussain, an insanely accomplished actor who played the titular role of Srikanta, was sitting beside me. I had learnt my lines and I knew not to look directly into the camera— that was the first piece of advice my mother had given me.

'Think of the camera as a boy you like. You want to impress him so you will offer him your best angle, you will make sure he can see and hear you but you will not address him directly. But you will always know where he is.' And so began my flirtation with the camera. At first it was a breathless, uncoordinated, clumsy affair that left me blushing to the roots of my hair, but gradually, over time, I relaxed—I learnt to exhale, to take my time, to bask in the camera's focused gaze.

And when the film ended I felt bereft. I called my mother from the airport in Kolkata, close to tears. I didn't understand why I felt so unanchored, so lost. She explained it was a natural reaction to being a part of a film—it's such an intense and personal experience, you give so much of yourself to playing a character for weeks and months, and then it all suddenly ends. And you have to learn to let go, to move on.

And so I moved on, albeit reluctantly. I had loved playing the cloistered and enigmatic Kamalata; the film's cast had become my closest friends; the unit felt like family. And now I was untethered, flapping feebly in the wind. What I needed was another film, another role to attach myself to.

Perhaps something more modern, more youthful— an energetic, driven girl, fresh out of college with the world at her feet, with dreams of a successful career and independence. In other words Neha from *Dil Maange More!!!*, my first Hindi film.

I wish someone had told me at the time that it was not wise to choose a film with three girls in it as your

Hindi debut—you must pick a film with a solo heroine, where it is all about you (after the hero, of course!). I was also asked to select from any of the three girls' roles that I liked best. I wish someone had told me to choose the girl who ends up with the boy. Instead, I simply heard the story and liked it and found the character of Neha to be the most compelling—someone who at eighteen is more keen on a prestigious job at an air hostess academy in the city than on marrying her college boyfriend and settling down in Samarpur, however idyllic a hill station it may be. How silly of me!

Movie mathematics is simple. One boy, three girls. Girl who chooses job over boy = vamp. Girl who chooses boy over everything else = heroine. And so I had in effect *chosen* not to be the heroine of my first commercial film.

The film's fate at the box office is well documented so there is no point in mincing words. It was a dud. As someone who had always excelled in everything I had done, this was uncharted territory—a failure, and a painfully public one at that. A popular national newspaper ran a review titled 'Dil Maange No More!' And it wasn't just the film that was criticized. As I scanned the scathing commentary for the section on performances, I saw my name followed by words that will be forever etched in my memory: 'She looks like her mother but she acts like her father.' Now Abba displayed some pretty decent acting chops on more than one occasion: Gwalior Suitings, Asian Paints, Lay's Chips, to name just a few advertisements he did, but I guess these had made no impression on the reviewer who obviously did not mean her statement as a compliment.

I was mortified. I had never failed at anything I had tried up to that point (except ballet) and here was a widely available, withering breakdown of my abilities or lack thereof.

'Don't read the reviews.' 'It's one person's opinion and often they're just having a bad day.' 'You can't make everyone happy.' This is what they tell you and there may be some actors who pay heed to that advice but the vast majority of us tend to painstakingly peruse every single online, print and electronic critique and rating.

Most actors who have stuck around long enough to see the inevitable downs that follow the ups sport the hide of a rhinoceros—but an unkind review can still jar to the bone and I had not yet had the time to grow a protective layer or two of thick skin. The last two paragraphs of the review swam before my eyes which had suddenly filled with unshed tears. I felt embarrassed and humiliated, singled out for public shaming. I didn't understand why they had to drag my family into it, why it couldn't be my failure alone. I couldn't bring myself to face anyone; I just wanted to shut myself off from the world until it had forgotten all about me.

I put my phone on silent, pulled the curtains shut and climbed into bed with a large tub of strawberry ice cream and the first season of *Sex and the City*. Eight hours and 6000 calories later, as the season credits rolled up my television screen, I felt emboldened by the global language of stilettos and funky crop tops. I was a strong, independent working woman and that reviewer was an unhappy frustrated jerk. I picked up my phone, ready to face a spate of sympathies or a torrent of taunts . . . There was one missed call from my driver and a message from Vodafone reminding me to pay my bill before the due date; not exactly the deluge of derision I had anticipated. I decided to hit the gym to try to repair some of the damage my binge fest had done.

Whilst on the treadmill I initially kept my head down and my eyes trained on my feet, assiduously avoiding eye contact with anyone. When I finally gathered the strength to glance around me, I expected to be greeted with smirks and sniggers but everyone was simply going about their normal fitness routines. My brother called me as I was walking out.

'Should we go out for dinner tonight?' he asked.

'My film is a disaster. They said I was a wooden doll with stilted dialogue delivery that sounded like I had been hit in the face,' I spewed, unable to control myself.

'Today's review lines tomorrow's waste-paper basket,' Bhai said breezily. 'People are going to say all sorts of things about you—good, bad and ugly. You can't take it to heart or you're going to want to bleed out in a tub of warm water. Pick you up at eight?'

He was right. I was going to have to learn not to care about what other people thought. I needed to commit to my work and accept that there would be some who would judge me, call me talentless or spoilt or inadequate. And that was okay—it didn't have to shatter my self-confidence, it didn't have to destroy my dreams. There will always be good and bad reviews, dream roles and lost opportunities, hits and misses at the box office. Success will never be final and failure will never be fatal. What matters is that you persevere.

My first Hindi film released in 2004, before today's age of ubiquitous social media. Today as I scroll through my Twitter feed it still amazes me how many people revel in hate, trolling public personalities they have never met and know nothing about. I myself have been a target of this on more than one occasion.

For instance, when I expressed my regret over former Reserve Bank of India governor Raghuram Rajan announcing his exit in June 2016.

My tweet read: 'Profound loss for India that RBI Gov #RaghuramRajan has been forced to exit. He can only help those who want to help themselves. Shame.'

These are some of the comments I was treated to:

'Does she know the full form of RBI?'
'Are we supposed to listen to dumb actresses now?'
'Why do you have to poke your long nose into everything? Stick to your area'

I am all for freedom of speech and fully respect that everyone has the right to an opinion but cyberbullying has become a fact of life and actors are often soft targets for anonymous vitriol. Most times it is best to ignore the comments but there are times when I feel compelled to rise to the bait.

In this case 140 characters were sufficient to frame an apt reply: 'LSE doesn't stand for the London School of Entertainment and "dumb actresses" are citizens with valid opinions on economic policy #nuffsaid.'

There are times, however, when the character limitation on Twitter does not allow for a mature and considered reaction. Such as when I was trolled more recently for wearing a sari. Yup, you read it right—not a bikini or a short skirt—both of which, incidentally, I have been photographed wearing in the past (as has my mother who was famously the first Indian actress to model a bikini on a magazine cover way back in the 1960s) but a six-metre traditional Kanjeevaram silk sari.

These are some of the milder comments worth repeating:

'So finally you have become a Hindu'

'Shame on you, you are not a Muslim'

'*Aap ye Khan surname lagana bandh kariye. Ye surname hamari hai, kaffiro ki nahin*' (Stop using Khan as a surname. It belongs to us, not to infidels)

The whole nine yards

At that moment 140 characters and all the emoticons in the world could not suffice in helping me express the indignation that swelled up inside me. Of course the comments belie an ignorance of religious customs and tradition—one has only to look to the sari-clad Muslim women of Bengal and South India to understand this. The issue, however, is a deeper and more troubling one. I am only one of millions of women who have been criticized for their choice of clothing and this particular sari incident reveals that the issue is not with an expression of sexuality or suggestive choices of apparel; it's about attacking a woman simply because she is a woman—plain old sexism. Every woman has the right to wear whatever she pleases and to even suggest otherwise is totally unacceptable. It's not the length of our hemlines that need to increase; it's the breadth of your minds.

A few days later I posted a picture of myself in a white dress printed with a motif of green leaves and took the

Leaf and let leaf

opportunity to make what I thought was a subtle point with the caption, 'Leaf and let leaf'. It's entirely possible no one made the connection but I felt pleased with myself!

In 2004 public criticism such as this may have crippled me, but today I can proudly display a dense and difficult-to-penetrate armour of thick skin which insulates me from insult. It has been diligently developed over the past thirteen years by regularly being outside of my comfort zone—playing roles that are far removed from who I am, performing complicated dance numbers live on stage, hosting game shows and interacting with strangers on an almost daily basis. I have acted in numerous films—some have earned critical and commercial acclaim, many could not achieve their full potential for various reasons and a few on whose release date I have felt compelled to leave the country.

Indisputably *Rang De Basanti* (2006) is my most successful film to date—both in terms of box office success as well as in terms of garnering me awards and credibility as an actor. It also remains the only film I had to audition for. I got a call from Rakeysh Omprakash Mehra's office to read for an integral part of an ensemble-cast film starring Aamir Khan to be produced by UTV. A.R. Rahman had already been signed as the music director and Binod Pradhan as the cinematographer. It was a dream project with a massive production budget of Rs 40 crore (in those days a whopping amount) and every young actor wanted to be a part of the cast. I remember enacting three scenes with Mehra cuing me himself. Two were light-hearted and breezy and one was my character Sonia's reaction to the announcement of the death of her fiancé Ajay (played by R. Madhavan) on national television.

The office had a sterile clinical environment with no props, no music to help create atmosphere. I had five minutes to centre myself and to imagine how I would react if I was to suddenly learn that the man I loved and was about to marry had died. It must have gone well because Mehra came up to me afterwards and said he wanted me to do exactly that when we shot the scene for real. And that scene is what finally won me the credibility that I sought as an actor.

With Bhai at the IIFA Awards in Leeds, UK

Upon its release *Rang De Basanti*, I am proud to say, broke all opening box office records in India. It was, at the time, the highest-grossing film in its opening weekend in India (Rs 23 crore) and had the highest opening day collection for a Bollywood film. The screenplay, dialogues, music and performances were all very well received and it went on to win the National Award for most popular film in 2007. The film is notable not only for its success but also for the impact it had on people's lives and attitudes;

in fact, the term 'RDB effect' was coined to describe the chord it struck with people.

For those of you who have not seen the film it is about a group of disillusioned, restless college students who reluctantly participate in a film on the political activities of militant revolutionaries led by Bhagat Singh and Chandra Shekhar Azad and who, after experiencing a personal tragedy, decide to take action, to fight for justice. The film cleverly illustrated the fact that one can be as revolutionary today as our national heroes of yesterday. The story seemed to tap into an angst, a cynicism with systemic corruption that people, especially the urban middle class and the youth of our country was harbouring.

Recalling the idealism of our own recent past it ignited a patriotism in the audience, an awakening, a sense of the need to take responsibility and to effect change. This was perhaps best displayed by the candlelight vigil that took place at India Gate after the Jessica Lal murder and the perceived legal injustice that ensued. The march was very much a mirror of the one led by the protagonists in RDB post Ajay's death. I do not want to exaggerate the popularity of the film or its influence on the desires and anxieties of the audience but RDB remains a film that will always hold a special place in my filmography for reasons beyond its profitability.

It is *Khoya Khoya Chand* (2007), however, that stands apart for me as my favourite film, my most memorable performance.

The movie was directed by Sudhir Mishra, and traces the rise and fall of an actress, Nikhat Sheikh, in the 1950s and is perhaps the most challenging role I have had the opportunity to perform.

One doesn't often get the chance to prep for months before a shoot, to really get into the skin of the character. I had to learn Urdu, Kathak, horse riding and sword fighting, among other skills, and that took time, although I readily admit I learnt the shortcut crash-course varieties!

Set life

When the film wrapped I felt empty, I felt I had given of myself in a way that I had never done before and I was drained but happy. It is very satisfying for an actor to feel that way. The film did not fare well at the box office and the reviews were mixed. This time I chose to dwell on the positive reviews and ignore the negative ones; I was proud of my work, and the fact that one of my strongest critics, my mother, loved me in the film meant the world to me.

I remember her coming up to me during the interval at the film premiere. 'You are so good,' she said. Just four words but I was overjoyed. I felt reaffirmed. Perhaps it wasn't going to be a disaster after all—this career choice, this left turn I had taken into the abyss.

Still from *Khoya Khoya Chand*

It has been ten years since then. I have been a part of good and not-so-good films; I have grown as an actor and now feel at ease in front of the camera, although I am aware that between 'action' and 'cut' my heart rate inevitably spikes but that is an adrenaline rush I relish and one that adds a necessary energy to my performance; I continue to read and watch reviews and acknowledge some if not all the mentions I get on social media.

There is something called the 'Celebrity Index' in a national newspaper which measures and ranks your fame relative to others. Fifty lucky actors and fifty plucky actresses make the cut every month, depending on their exploits, film-related and otherwise. I myself am living on borrowed time—having featured at a modestly moderate 26 in July 2016, to hitting a personal best of 18 in September (during the *31st October* film promotions) and being currently dangerously close to being ousted at 46, a precarious position I know.

It brings one fact into sharp focus: People will say negative things about you personally as well as criticize your work but over time you realize that the worst responses are not the disparaging ones, it's when they don't respond at all—when you're simply not relevant enough to be discussed. Perhaps my being a student of history helps me reconcile an actor's desire for fame with a fear of being forgotten—I am aware that no matter how much notability and prestige you garner in your career, in the larger scheme of things most of us will be consigned to oblivion. In the absence of this understanding it is easy to get caught up in a desire for prominence which breeds a competition for attention that can be intense and claustrophobic.

Life as an actor can be stifling. Our Hindi film industry is prolific—producing more films than any other in the world. Every third person in the gym wants to be a hero/heroine—the competition is intense, and envy and insecurity, rife. It is easy to feel validated or destroyed by other people's opinions and living on the surface becomes a simpler, more appealing option. It becomes easier to scroll through Instagram judging people by the way they look instead of delving deeper. And consequently it becomes more important to look good.

Shortcut options are popular now: steroids to sculpt one's body, instead of proper diet; muscle-building and cardiovascular exercises to burn fat. Cosmetic enhancements such as Botox, fillers and tummy tucks are now as mundane as waxing your legs. One just does what it takes to look good. Relationships too seem to survive only on the surface, with an emphasis on having fun and living in the moment. It is too tedious to share our deepest feelings, too hard to commit to being there when things get tough, too demanding to learn from our mistakes.

If we are unwilling to dig deeper within ourselves to get in touch with our dreams and fears, we are unlikely to give that chance to our friends. So much so that people have stopped really knowing each other or impacting each other's lives. It is more of an existence and less of a life, a life more empty than full.

The irony is that as an actor you are required to dig deep and unearth emotions, to empathize with the characters you play on screen. But how can you do that honestly if you are convinced the world revolves around you? If, like Mercator, you have not stepped out to experience the world in all its diversity and magnificence? That is why it is essential to take the plunge and dive deep. Move outside of your comfort zone. Test yourself. Learn to live and love completely. And one of the best ways to do that is to pack a bag and get out of Bollywood. Remind yourself of the tiny speck you are in the universe.

Because if you continue to live on the surface you will flatline.

7

We'll Always Have Paris

'We won't go unless you are absolutely ready. But when I say go, you run. Don't look back and for God's sake don't hesitate.'

You would be forgiven for thinking these are dialogues from the epic 1963 American film *The Great Escape*, spoken by actor Steve McQueen to a nervous prisoner of war about to embark on a daring escape from a high-security Nazi war camp. In actuality they were said by Tom to me as I sat dangling my legs over the guard rail that acts as a protective boundary to keep vehicles from straying off the road. We were stranded somewhere on the M25, one of England's busiest motorways—a dual four-lane roadway—that encircles almost all of Greater London and is used by hundreds of thousands of cars every day. It was a beautiful spring day in March 1997 and we were hitch-hiking from Oxford to Paris as part of a university cancer-awareness fundraiser.

With Tom on the ferry from Spain to Morocco

Up until then we had fared incredibly well, having traversed a little more than half the distance to Dover (150 miles from Oxford) where we would catch the ferry to Calais. We had got lifts from a man on his way to work, a woman dropping her children to school (who gave us sandwiches), and the driver of a massive juggernaut who very kindly got on his CB radio to spread the news that he had two passengers on a cross-country voyage in need of assistance. There was a flurry of favourable responses to his announcement, which I suspect had something to do with his description of us as two scantily clad buxom Scandinavian damsels in distress! A man promptly and very generously assured him he would take us all the way to Canterbury, a mere 20 miles from Dover. When he saw a decidedly un-female Tom and un-Norse me climbing out of the lorry he managed to mask his disappointment but 10 miles into the journey, he had a sudden change of heart and unceremoniously dropped us on a slip road in the middle of nowhere.

And so there we were, stranded on the wrong side of the M25 with vehicles zipping up and down the eight lanes between us and where we needed to get. We had no option but to make a dash for it. That or wait to be picked up by a police car.

I bent down to retie my shoelaces, adjusted my backpack and studied the stream of hurtling cars warily, awaiting Tom's command. I didn't look for a gap in the traffic but focused instead on Tom's voice—he had to yell to be heard over the whoosh of rushing automobiles—and when he shouted, 'GO!' I ran. It was exhilarating. Liberating. And stupid. So stupid. But also so exhilarating. Nothing like a brush with death to make you feel alive! We walked for an hour or two after that, at first along the motorway and then down a side road, through quaint English villages. We had lunch in a pub that spilled out on to a green where a cricket game was afoot. We talked about what pizzas we liked: me, the cheesy deep pan sort you could sink your teeth into; Tom, the thin crust powdery kind that snaps between your fingers like a biscuit. We passed churches with clanging bells and farms full of cattle, pigs and chickens. We crossed small streams and thatched homes with attached gardens. I was worried we were falling behind in the race but Tom was unperturbed. 'The good traveller has no fixed plans,' he said, 'and is not intent on arriving.' He told me later that he had been quoting from *The Art of Travel* by Alain de Botton but then I was overwhelmed by what I had assumed was his wisdom. At some point it started to rain but we walked on, our faces turned up to the open skies, catching droplets on our tongues, laughing with reckless abandon.

It was early evening and the sky was beginning to turn pink when we finally flagged down a passing car. The driver was a middle-aged woman who was initially suspicious of us but upon learning about the hitch-hike's cancer-awareness goals decided to go an hour out of her way to drive us all the way to Dover. It transpired that her mother had recently lost a painful battle against lung cancer and she was very appreciative of our efforts. We arrived in Dover around 8 p.m. and managed to get on the ferry shortly after. It had taken us twelve hours to travel the 150 miles between Oxford and Dover but it had been such an adventure—and there was more in store.

When the ferry arrived in Calais at 10.30 p.m. we spilled out on to the dock with the rest of the passengers—

groups of families, traders and other travellers—who then started to disperse one by one, getting into their cars, hailing cabs or walking away . . . until only Tom and I were left. We had approached several of the passengers, asking for rides to Paris, but sadly there had been no takers. Now you may recall that Tom and I had only met at the start of university, six months before this jolly jaunt. Tom would later go on to set up the global activist group Avaaz, and currently runs UK foreign policy on Syria, Iraq and ISIS. But that public-spirited, responsible streak wasn't entirely evident back then and though we were friends, finding myself all alone in the middle of the night in a desolate and foreign part of the world with a nineteen-year-old boy, my sense of self-preservation and suspicion was heightened.

I sneaked a glance at Tom from the corner of my eye whilst my brain tried fervently to remember the French word for 'Help'! Thanks to the British School I had a GCSE in French and could confidently name twenty kinds of farm animals, the main parts of the human body and count to one hundred—all being of immense practical import of course! Thankfully, Tom seemed uninterested in assaulting me and announced gaily that he had a plan. We walked the short distance to Calais Ville Railway Station intending to hop on to a fast TGV train to cover the remaining 180 miles to Paris in under an hour. If we were lucky we would reach our destination, the Eiffel Tower, before the clock struck midnight.

But we were not lucky. The station was shut and the sign on the door said it would open only at 4.30 a.m.—six hours later. And that is how I came to spend my first, and only, night sleeping on a city pavement. I use 'sleeping' in the loosest sense of the word in that I was lying down but my eyes and ears were alert to every tiny movement in the dark. Was that a paper bag blowing in the breeze, a rat foraging for food or a homicidal maniac intent on murdering me for my leftover cheese sandwich? I couldn't tell if I was trembling with fear, shivering because of the cold or simply shaking from the reverberations of Tom's buzz-saw snoring, but I didn't sleep a wink.

We were the first people in the station when the doors opened. And as the inky night sky surrendered to the golden-pink rays of the rising sun, our train finally pulled into Gare du Nord. All the participants of the hitch-hike were to meet under the Eiffel Tower at 8 p.m. to take the bus home to Oxford which gave Tom and me about twelve hours in Paris.

'The best way to discover a city is by foot,' Tom declared, and set off at a brisk pace in what he had deduced was the direction of the Seine (how did he know?). What followed was one of the most glorious days of my life. We bought baguettes and cheese and had a picnic by the river. I never knew such an innocuous mix of flour, water and yeast could taste so wonderful—fresh, fragrant and utterly sustaining.

We walked across one of the thirty-seven bridges linking the left and right banks of the Seine—it was to become my favourite, the magnificent golden Pont Alexandre III. As we started up the Champs-Élysées, arguably the most beautiful avenue in the world, I remarked to Tom that I had been here before.

'Let's do this differently then,' he said and held me firmly by the shoulders. He looked searchingly into my eyes, 'Do you trust me?'

'Not really,' my brain proffered but politeness prevailed and instead I said, 'Sure.'

'Close your eyes and let me guide you. I'll tell you when to turn, when to stop, when to cross the road.'

I looked at Tom, then looked at the wide 2-kilometre-long avenue lined with shops, cafes, restaurants and teeming with people. I looked back at Tom incredulously.

'Trust me,' he said. It struck me that I had already placed my faith in him by agreeing to go on the hitch-hike and following his lead—and we had survived more than one sticky situation together.

We must have looked a strange sight: me, eyes squeezed shut and hands held out for balance, and Tom, firing urgent instructions as we weaved our way towards the Arc de Triomphe, that stands at the western end of the Champs-Élysées—peculiar perambulatory partners. Halfway there we swapped positions and I led Tom the rest of the way, faltering at first but slowly gaining confidence. At the time I was intent on the exercise, absorbed in not stumbling; it was only much later, during the bus ride home, that I realized that during that 2-kilometre walk Tom had subtly handed over the reins to me, and I had taken them.

Up until university I had had a very sheltered childhood—the same school and the same friends, the same six-week annual summer holiday to England. It was time for the frog to hop out of the well. It was early days but I was on my first unsupervised journey and I was finding my own way.

We spent the rest of the afternoon climbing Montmartre all the way up to the gleaming basilica of Sacré-Cœur, one of the highest points in Paris, offering a breathtaking panoramic view of the city. On the way down we stumbled across a tiny Salvador Dali museum, tucked away at the end of a cobbled street. It housed some of the lesser-known works of the eccentric artist, especially a number of his whimsical melting clocks—both alluring and grotesque. It was an opportune reminder of the passage of time and the need to meet the rest of our group at the appointed hour.

An hour later I found myself standing underneath the 'Tour Eiffel', the iconic iron lattice tower that forms the tallest structure in Paris and is also the most-visited paid monument in the world. And for good reason. We've all seen pictures of it but when you are standing underneath it, looking up at its triangulated wrought-iron frame rising up to a massive 985 feet, you can't help but feel overcome by its grandeur. At night this grandeur is enhanced with a golden glow that emanates from powerful yellow sodium lamps positioned at the base of the tower.

From the turn of the century, 20,000 sparkling lights have been superimposed over the golden lighting which bring the tower to life every hour on the hour for five minutes from sundown to 1 a.m. Because each of these lights has been installed individually, they flicker on and off at random, simulating sparkling stars. It is quite simply magical. I have felt dwarfed before—I'm all of five feet two inches and I come from a family of overachievers—but the humility you feel

All that glitters

when you are confronted with the sublime, be it natural or man-made, is one that everyone should experience.

I settled back into my seat on the bus home, exhausted but happy. My mind turned to the essay I had to submit on the impact of Darwin on the writing of history; I also had to remember to pick up fresh milk for my coffee the next morning. As I turned my face away from the city of lights and readied myself for the journey home, Tom's sleepy voice wafted up to me, 'It's always been a dream of mine to run naked through the sand dunes. Have you ever been to Africa?'

And so a year later, in the spring of 1998—when Celine Dion's 'My Heart Will Go On' was topping the UK charts—Tom, Alison (an American student in her first year at Balliol) and I flew to Spain, where we spent two weeks backpacking around Madrid, Toledo, Córdoba, Seville and Granada. We then took a ferry across the Strait of Gibraltar to cover the short distance from Tarifa in Spain to Tangier in Morocco, a ninety-minute journey at the most. My memories of that holiday alone could fill the pages of this book and are impossible to do justice to in a single chapter but I will try to share some of the highlights.

Picture a hut made out of hardened clay, its roof consisting of dry vegetation—straw of some kind in all probability. There is no furniture inside the hut, only a couple of sleeping mats, a stove and a few extra clothes hanging on a line. The hut is in Mohamet, the last remote Berber settlement before the ever-expanding Sahara. It belonged to Abdul, an indigenous nomad who had agreed to be our guide on a four-day-three-night camel trek into the 3000-mile sweep of desert.

Berber hospitality

This is where Tom, Alison and I spent the night before we began our intrepid adventure. We ate on the floor by candlelight as the village was not electrified—a feast of tagine (stew) and couscous after which Abdul told us stories of growing up in the desert over glasses of 'whisky berber' (sweet mint tea). Because we didn't know any Arabic he spoke to us in French and very broken English.

We decided to sleep early and set off at dawn, intending to get five or six hours of trek in before it became too hot.

Tom and Alison were experienced travellers, well equipped with sleeping bags which they promptly climbed into and fell asleep; I had not had much occasion to sleep outside of a bed and so had no sleeping bag. I lay on the floor of the hut, watching the one remaining candle burn out, the wax dripping down its sides to form a little puddle at the base. There must have been a breeze because the yellow flame was dancing, casting shadows on the walls, making them seem alive. And then I realized that the walls did not seem alive, they were alive—teeming with hundreds of insects. They were everywhere.

Some were shiny and beetle-like, scurrying up and down the walls intent on their nocturnal missions; others were larger with long furry appendages stumbling about drunkenly. My gaze was drawn to a particularly icky sort: a dark brown fellow with short antennae and two pairs of membranous wings, hanging upside down from the ceiling directly above me. His big bug eyes set wide apart seemed to be trained on me and, as I stared back in horror, he unfurled his translucent wings as if in slow motion, ready to take flight . . . Just then the candle flickered desperately, grew faint and went out, leaving me in a darkness that was claustrophobic in its completeness. You guessed it—I didn't sleep a wink that night.

It was still dark when Abdul called to us from outside the hut, '*Viens recontrer tes chameux.*' Come meet your camels. Tom and Alison were thrilled and ran out without hesitation. I was unimpressed—we have camels in India. I had sat on them enough times on school trips to Rajasthan and once during a wedding in Udaipur. In fact I expected to be relatively unmoved during this entire excursion, having grown up surrounded by what my Western friends no doubt thought were the style and affectations of 'the Orient'. So I played it cool—much like the previous evening when we were choosing our headscarves for the journey.

Abdul had held out scarves of all colours that we were to fashion into turbans to protect our heads from the sun and prevent heatstroke. Tom and Alison had sensibly chosen white, a colour known to absorb less heat than darker hues. Now, I grew up in Delhi where temperatures as high as 48 degrees Celsius have been recorded; I wasn't

Two minutes before sunstroke set in

about to let a little desert calefaction faze me. So I chose one of my favourite colours, a deep navy blue.

When I emerged, Tom and Alison had already mounted their chosen steeds, Arfa and Ixa. Which left Humpy Thing for me. And Humpy Thing was unlike any camel I had seen back home. Firstly he was huge—over 7 feet long from nose to tail and probably about 9 feet high from the ground to his hump. And his hump was gigantic. There was no box to sit on like there is in India, in fact there was no cushioning at all save a well-worn rug thrown carelessly across his back. My confidence faltered as I tried to clamber on as gracefully as I could. It was impossible to sit comfortably and try as I might I simply could not get my legs around his massive hump. I ended up perched precariously, clinging on to a small rope extending from his swanlike neck. When dawn broke, our procession lurched forward.

Sahara sojourn

As I held on for dear life I sneaked a peek at Tom who was atop Ixa, reading from *1001 Arabian Nights* and looking tremendously tranquil. We rode for five hours until the sun was directly above us, beating down mercilessly. There was not a cloud in the sky or a tree to provide even a sliver of shade. It was like being slowly cooked in a giant oven. The rhythmic sway of Humpy Thing, my lack of sleep, and the intense heat were making me dizzy and before I fainted dead away I called to Abdul to stop. Tom helped me down from my perch and Alison ripped the ridiculous almost-black turban from my pounding head. I let them put a damp cloth on my forehead and give me small sips of water to drink. After a few minutes I felt strong enough to open my eyes.

Humpy Thing was watching me with his large dark eyes fringed by impossibly thick eyelashes, a necessary

Humpy Thing

protection from the dust I would later learn. There was an expression of stoic resignation in those eyes but behind the phlegmatism there seemed to lurk a hint of amusement, a mischievous sparkle. It was probably my sunstroked mind playing tricks on me but I could have sworn my camel was scoffing at me. So much for my foreign fortitude!

Our Sahara sojourn lasted four days and three nights and was one of the most challenging, breathtaking and memorable holidays of my life. We fell into a pattern of riding from dawn to about 11 a.m. and then from around 3 p.m. to nightfall. If the days were searing, the lack of humidity caused the night-time temperatures to plunge to freezing. We ate sparingly—tagines and biscuits mostly—and partook of our limited supply of water prudently. Yet we ran out of water by noon on the fourth day, six hours from our final destination. I am fortunate never to have felt a hunger or thirst that wasn't self-imposed

Soha of Arabia

but in those six hours I felt a disabling sense of anxiety bordering on panic.

Tom cheerfully declared that the human body can survive three full days without water but that, unsurprisingly, did nothing to ebb my unease. It was only when we were back in Mohamet and I had a glass of deliciously crisp ice-cold H_2O in my hand that I felt calmed.

Looking for a Starbucks

Perhaps the most afraid I have ever been was when I needed to go to the loo one night. We had camped in a field of sand dunes piled up in mounds and ridges as far as the eye could see. I decided to walk behind a couple of the larger ones for maximum privacy. When I was done I retraced my steps expecting to see the others after I rounded a particularly serpentine dune but instead I was confronted with another dune. I looked to my right and then to my left but in the dark all the dunes looked identical. I was instantly and completely lost in a sea of silvery sand, phosphorescent from the luminous moon, its cresting waves frozen in time. There was no way of knowing which direction I had come from and the danger of aimlessly going around in circles was very real. I recalled Abdul's story of an American tourist who strayed too far from his camp and got disoriented. He was only 350 metres from the camp when he was found four hours later—an hour too late. Thankfully my reverie was broken by the sound of Abdul's voice calling my name. I answered gratefully, blinking back tears of relief, and shortly after we were reunited. From then on every time I had to answer the call of nature I made Alison come with me. Survival trumps privacy any day!

At night when we slept, the threadbare rug atop Humpy Thing, which saved my posterior from second-degree friction burns during the day, served as my mattress. As a child in Pataudi, I remember we would move our mosquito-netted beds into the courtyard when it got too hot. This was before we had air conditioners installed. We would sleep underneath the stars and try to discern various constellations. My name, Soha, means 'star' in Arabic, specifically a star in the Great Bear and I cannot look up at a starry sky without trying to find me. As I lay on the sand in the middle of the Sahara, feeling lost and vulnerable to the elements, I looked for my namesake in the sky and there it was—small but bright and burning fiercely. I felt anchored and reassured.

On our third and last night I had fallen asleep staring at the infinite expanse of the universe, wondering if we were really all alone in it or not. Either way it boggled the mind. I don't know what woke me but I opened my eyes to find Abdul leaning over me, his face inches from mine. He was grinning down at me and I could count the brown stains on his two front teeth. 'What do you want?' I asked sitting up to put some space between us. Abdul continued to smile broadly. I looked for Tom for assistance but realized that his sleeping bag was empty and he was nowhere to be seen. I felt panic rising within me. How could we have been so foolish as to entrust our lives to a complete stranger, to allow him to lead us, defenceless, into the middle of a completely uninhabited region. He had obviously murdered Tom and was about to have his evil way with me.

'*Viens avec moi*,' Abdul whispered. Come with me. Not a chance, I thought to myself looking for Alison. I could see her blonde hair spilling out through the zip of the sleeping bag but I couldn't tell if she was moving, breathing. Abdul got to his feet, gesturing to me to follow him. To this day I don't know why I obeyed; perhaps I wanted to appear compliant until I could uncover some sort of weapon to overpower him with. It would have to be one that could subdue but not kill because the latter would leave me all alone in the middle of the largest desert in the world—not the best plan. We climbed together to the top of a sickle-shaped dune and I looked at my Berber guide, awaiting further instruction. He was staring straight ahead, beaming like a Cheshire cat. I followed his gaze: It was Tom, running full speed between two dunes, arms held high over his head—naked as a newborn baby!

Tom had had a dream that most would have dismissed as crazy but he made it happen. He showed me that dreams didn't have to be futile. He helped me expand my horizons. I was eighteen when I hitch-hiked to Paris with him, but I was not new to travelling. Even then my passport carried visas for the United Kingdom, the United States, Switzerland, Singapore among others . . . France too. But each of those trips had been orchestrated, supervised, sanitized. Travel is meant to take you out of the familiar and into the unknown, out of your comfort zone into murky waters, out of your cocoon into a new and exciting world—it is meant to be an education. You learn about new cultures, ways of living, eating, loving, ways different to yours; about yourself, your limits, physical and mental, and your openness to new ideas.

What then is the best way to travel—and must it involve risking one's life by dashing across busy motorways and/or exposing oneself to potentially venomous insects as you lie shivering on the floor of a strange man's hut while waiting for the sun to come up? If we can assume that a primary life goal for most people is to have adventure, then yes, it is important to let go—of schedule, of comfort, of trepidation. It may not always be fun, but we seek the perspective that distance and change can give.

We travel because we know we will come home and when we do, home is the same but we are changed and that changes everything. When I look up at the night sky from my terrace in Mumbai today, it is not mundane and boring, but full of infinite possibility—it is after all the very same night sky that filled me with wonder in Africa.

Travel has taught me many valuable life lessons but the one that is most pertinent is of acceptance. I am following in the footsteps of superstars and reprobation is an ever-present risk. It is not unusual for me to feel inadequate, to feel frustrated, to feel that no matter what I achieve, in comparison to my parents, my brother, I will always fall short. But when you are standing on the edge of the spectacular Grand Canyon for instance and

The majestic Grand Canyon

looking into its plunging depths, containing over two billion years of geographical history, you cannot help but feel diminished by the world.

There is so much out there that is bigger than you, stronger than you and that will endure long after you are gone, it inspires you to accept your flaws, your mortality and the fact that not everything will bend to your will. If you really want to know what grounds me—a modern-day princess from a tremendously famous family—it is this awareness.

In 2009 I found myself back in Paris, dressed in bright orange janitor overalls, broom in hand, attempting

After being turned away from the Louis Vuitton store in Paris

impossibly complicated choreographed dance moves with Shreyas Talpade for a film called 'Chemistry' (a film that was such a heady cocktail of bad writing and amateur direction that, true to its name, it spontaneously combusted pre-release). As the song lyrics—'You and me, Babyyyy, we got chemistreee, you and me'—blared over the Champ de Mars, I watched the choreographer and his assistant perform the steps we were to duplicate.

Inured by years of experience, they seemed oblivious to the crowds of tourists stopping to take in the spectacle. When it was time for the shot I got up to take my position in front of the camera. In my line of sight there was an Indian family, their backs squarely to the Eiffel Tower, one of the seven new wonders of the world, taking photographs of us instead. To my right there was a group of backpackers poring over a city map and arguing over where to go next. How lucky I was to have once been one of them, I thought to myself as the music kicked in. And not just Paris or Morocco—I had since learnt how to cook pasta in a rented villa in Tuscany, had buckets of soapy water chucked at me in a traditional hammam in Istanbul and watched two lions copulate an arm's length from me in a national park in South Africa.

My eyes came to rest on a couple embracing under the Tower: The girl was wiping away her tears whilst the boy looked visibly relieved and somewhat overwhelmed. It was obvious that he had proposed to her, and she had accepted. As Adil, the choreographer, counted in the beats . . . 5 . . . 6 . . . 7 . . . 8 . . . and I summoned up the terpsichorean inside me, little did I know that five years and six months later, in July 2014, I would be back in Paris in that very spot under the Eiffel Tower, watching Kunal produce the most perfect ring in the world and ask me to be his wife. But that is the subject of another chapter.

Yes, a thousand times Yes

It's Complicated

I have sat down to write this chapter seventeen times.

I look at old photographs, read through my diaries and letters, watch my wedding video. I look at Kunal's boyishly beautiful face as he sits across the room from me, scrolling through his Facebook newsfeed. He has such a defined jawline. And his forearms are so sinewy that when he moves his fingers to type something into his phone I can see his muscles flex.

And then, just when I'm feeling it, a blossoming of passion inside me that radiates to my very fingertips as they prepare to fly across the keyboard, spilling our story of love, he does something that makes me want to get up and punch him in the face.

Like now. We agreed to spend the first half of the day writing in the study and so here I am, poised at my computer. Kunal has been glued to his phone for over an hour. I look at the clock. It's 11.15 a.m. It's not healthy to be at a screen for so long, so early in the morning. Every so often there is a staccato burst of noise from the phone—a video someone has posted of their dog howling 'I love you', the latest remix song from a recent film, a new dialogue promo. It's hard to concentrate on writing.

I can see his newest meticulously researched purchase, a pair of high-tech headphones, in the tray just by his outstretched legs. Maybe if I look at him meaningfully he'll take the hint and put them on.

Except he hasn't looked up even once in the last thirty-five minutes. And now he has found an instruction video on how to tune your guitar. If he reaches for his guitar I will have to throw something at him.

Thankfully a solution presents itself to me just as my hand closes over the oxidizing apple core left over from breakfast. I put on the noise-cancelling headphones he has not thought to wear and am immediately and blissfully cut off from all ambient sound.

Where was I? Love. Light brown eyes that crinkle up with laughter and a full mouth with the power to hypnotize. I sneak another look at the love of my life . . . who is now scribbling something in my daily planner, which I have told him only a million times not to do. The least he can do is write on the dates that have passed and not on those yet to come! I swallow an internal surge of exasperation, take off the headphones and join him on the couch where we proceed to watch three episodes of 'Line of Duty' on Netflix.

Love.

I remember Mrs Narula, my literature teacher in Year 6 of the British School, telling us to read a Mills and Boon novel. We were going to study 'romantic love'—everything from Chaucer's 'The Miller's Tale' to Byron's epic satire *Don Juan* to Jane Austen's *Pride and Prejudice*—and the Mills and Boon would be the perfect primer to break us in. If you are a girl then surely you've read at least one Mills and Boon novel? They continue to be the most popular publishers of romantic fiction escapist fantasy books. So popular in fact that during the Second World War when paper was rationed, Mills and Boon books were allowed to be printed to boost the morale of women! The love stories are a tad formulaic—girl meets boy, girl finds boy arrogant and unfeeling, boy seduces girl somewhat against her will (disturbingly bordering on rape), a burning desire for boy is ignited inside girl, who (blinded by a heady cocktail of serotonin, dopamine and oxytocin) sees boy in new light as kind and misunderstood, boy admits his love for girl in an ego-swallowing feat that almost kills him, girl and boy embrace and ride off into a perfect sunset. I had read one or two already, notably *Stranded, Seduced, Pregnant* (real title) and *Bootie and the Beast* (okay, this is borrowed) with a particularly steamy cover that I concealed in a jacket made out of old newspaper. I couldn't believe these guilty pleasures were now part of my official academic syllabus!

As a young girl picking her way through the minefield that is adolescence, these books must have cast their impression on my putty-like brain. Adonis-like chiselled heroes who were wealthy, powerful brutes; helpless heroines who were young, feisty and painfully bountiful . . . er . . . beautiful. Simmering sexual tension which would inevitably explode into the most perfect and tender love that always ended happily, if not in marriage then in a firm commitment to be together. Putting aside a feminist critique of the desirability of these gender stereotypes, a brief glance at the boys in my literature class would have demonstrated that these characters were in fact far from real and the world within the pages a fantasy. Not every girl wants to be rescued and not every boy is the ideal blend of demanding and commanding.

Mrs Narula, with all her experience and wisdom, broke it down for us—if we harboured expectations about love as portrayed in these and other romantic novels, we would be setting ourselves up for disappointment and regret. 'Perfection,' she said in her very matter-of-fact way, 'simply does not exist.'

It may seem an obvious statement, nothing really staggering there, but I do feel that when we read a romance novel or watch a romantic comedy we tend to look over at our partners and wonder when the last time was that they bought us flowers or chocolates or professed their love for us through some grand gesture. Chances are, if your partner is like mine, that his proposal of marriage to you will leap to mind. And then you will remember all the time that has passed since, multiple anniversaries even, and nothing of romantic import will strike you. And then you will bring up the fact that he still hasn't written on the card for your cousin's wedding, to which he will say he hardly knows your cousin and that you haven't left much room for him on the card anyway so you might as well sign his name, and before you know it you will be arguing about how he doesn't pull his weight around the house and a perfectly good evening will be ruined.

Love is certainly the most precious and cherished thing but it is not all lingering looks and amorous embraces. It is not the ability to know what the other person needs without them actually having to tell you. It is not the absence of irritation, conflict or disappointment. It is hard work and there is always room for improvement. Mrs Narula was not the only person to give the teenage me a lesson in realism.

When I left for university at seventeen, Amman sat me down and said, 'You will need to learn about a lot of things—how to use a washing machine, how to cook, how to operate a bank account, sex, how to take public transport . . .' Whoa! That was the first time she had ever mentioned the word 'sex' to me, benignly sandwiched as it was between mundane chores. She looked at me intently and said something which at the time I found a little shocking coming from a parent, but in hindsight it was some of the best advice a mother can give her daughter.

'Just because you have sex with someone, doesn't mean you have to marry them. Sex can muddy the brain and make you feel things like trust and empathy. You may think you're in love but you may not be.' Those three sentences seemed to take the wind out of her and I thought for a second she was going to cry but she got up, straightened the bedcover and said, 'You're also going to have to learn to make your own bed.'

End of talk.

At the time I had had a grand total of two boyfriends—both from my class, both well known to my parents, and both really just friends who were boys you could count on to ask you to slow dance to 'With or Without You' by U2. But my first memory of finding a boy attractive was way back in school when I was seven. Daniel was blonde and blue-eyed and I was always really giggly in his company. When it was announced that the class play was *Sleeping Beauty* and Daniel would play the role of the Prince, I prayed fervently to be cast as Princess Aurora. It was not to be though and I watched bitterly from the wings as my classmate Savitri got kissed on the cheek by him. It didn't require much acting for me to play my part—a grouchy goblin goon.

Daniel's family moved away from Delhi shortly after and I was inconsolable for two whole days. However, the resilience of youth saw me bounce back from this, my first experience of unrequited love. Thankfully the pursuant years were consumed by forceful feelings of the opposite sex being gross and yucky, wretched specimens who pulled your hair and rubbed their snot on your dresses.

My second bout of unrequited love would be many years later, at fifteen. Let's not give this person a name because I never told him I liked him and I would like to keep it that way. He was a boy in my sister Saba's class, so two years my senior, and he was 'bad news'. He had long hair and dressed scruffily, bunked class, had been caught smoking in the bicycle shed and held the record for most suspensions from school. And I was drawn to him like a moth to a flame. Or more accurately a moth afflicted by paralysis because I never actually got close enough to get burnt. Instead I stalked him happily from a distance, content to stare at him from across the basketball court or, if I was lucky, to pass him in the corridor and mumble a strangled 'Hey'. You couldn't convince me it wasn't love, a love that lasted for eight whole months until said person graduated and went off to college in America. This time I nursed my broken heart for a full week before the distraction of our class trip to Mount Abu and Udaipur. By the time I came back from that I had forgotten all about what's-his-name.

So I can safely say that in matters of the heart, when I left for university, at the threshold of adulthood, I was well-armed with good advice from Amman and Mrs Narula but poorly equipped in experience. Since then I have been to two colleges where I got my BA and MSc degrees, I have attended too many ABBA-themed retro parties, travelled, discovered make-up and hair removal, met boys whom I actually had conversations with—some were interesting, some dull—I have broken a few hearts, had my heart broken, worked in different industries, made new friends and lost touch with old ones . . . in short I have lived my life. There were perhaps two relationships in this time that stand out. It would be crude and unfair to the other people involved to divulge the specifics but I would like to share some of what I learnt, as tactfully and graciously as possible.

JC was my best friend at Oxford. I met him in my first year, in the second month of the first term, and we were together until well after we graduated, when the cruel fingers of long-distance tore us apart—aka the relationship became mutually inconvenient and we met other people. He was . . . unconventional.

The first time we met was when he knocked on my door one evening, asking to borrow some blue eyeshadow, preferably glitter-based, for a party he was on his way to. He was wearing fishnet stockings, a tank top and a miniskirt. As I applied the eyeshadow for him, I inquired innocently if the party he was going to had a fancy-dress theme. 'No,' he said, and bounded out the door leaving me with my mouth agape. I think it was curiosity that made me seek him out over the next few days. He was not gay. He was expressive and enjoyed making what he called 'postmodern artistic statements'. He made me laugh; in fact he was an amateur stand-up comic so he made lots of people laugh. He played the mandolin, wrote songs and was a left-arm spinner on the cricket team. He was also a devout born-again Christian (to be 'born-again' means you have experienced a spiritual rebirth as separate from your physical birth and now have a personal relationship with Jesus Christ). He introduced me to Leonard Cohen, Jeff Buckley and the Smashing Pumpkins. Our negatively reinforced maturity levels would result in wholesome activities like playing badminton across the quad with a blueberry muffin and ten-pin bowling down aisles of the local supermarket with an onion and some tubes of toothpaste. He didn't care a hoot for what people thought about him—whether they booed him on stage during a comedy gig or whether they mocked him for his religious beliefs or his unusual sense of fashion. He was who he was and he taught me that it was okay to be who I was. If I wasn't a big drinker I didn't have to drink to have fun, if I was shy and took time to open up to people that was fine too (although it probably wasn't okay to have a giant Twix and a Diet Coke for lunch every day). JC helped me come out of my shell in a foreign land and when we parted three years later at the end of college we said we would stay in touch. I moved back to Delhi and got a job at the Ford Foundation, an international NGO headquartered in New York, with the global mission of advancing human welfare—economic empowerment, education, human rights and democracy.

The first sign of concern for me was when I called JC to tell him I had secured this amazing job and his response to me was that it was like 'polishing the brass on the Titanic'. When I pressed him to explain, he said these people we were helping were sinking ships and what they needed was for someone to save their souls, not give them a sandwich. It was what he truly believed and I knew then that even though we were best friends who had the most fun together, we were not going to be together. And then the sign-off on his emails changed, from 'Love, JC' to 'Your brother in Christ, JC'. It wasn't that I was losing a potential life partner; I was only twenty-one and I knew I had my whole life ahead of me, but I was losing my best friend.

Cut to, as we film folk like to say, 2002, the bar at the Imperial Hotel in New Delhi. I was back from the London School of Economics and Political Science, having done my MSc in International Relations (not International Relationships as the media here so often misquotes, a degree they have not instituted as yet but one focused on honing, I would imagine, a wholly different skill set!). I had secured a job as an associate banker at Citigroup Private Bank in London and it was to begin with a year's training at the bank's Mumbai office. I had a fortnight to kill before I was due to leave Delhi and was spending most nights out with friends. I was standing by the doors that led out on to the garden, discussing where we could go next with my gang of girls, when he entered the room. Tall, dark and handsome. Textbook good looks.

I tried to drag my eyes away from him as he walked over to join his friends two tables away from us. My friend Meher was saying something to me but I couldn't concentrate on her words, I was only aware, acutely, of the presence of this man and the blood rushing in my ears. Perhaps I willed it but he looked over at me then and held my unwavering gaze. I could feel my face turning red but he offered up an easy open smile and I smiled shyly back. The rest of the evening passed in a daze of distraction but, as we were gathering up our things to leave, I saw him approach us from the corner of my eye. I can't remember exactly what was said but I do remember the euphoria and the relief washing over me when he took my number and asked if he could call me sometime.

The next few days were a blur of phone calls, coffee dates, dinner engagements and parties. DJ seemed more mature than the other boys I knew—he drove a car, had a job, a beard even. I was used to being friends with someone and that friendship slowly developing into something more; this was the opposite and it was new and thrilling. In what seemed like the blink of an eye, my two weeks were up and it was time for me to pack my bags and move to Mumbai. It was DJ's optimism, his unshakeable resolve that fuelled my belief that we could make it work. He even bought me a ring as proof of his commitment but my mother made me return it, saying it was too early to accept presents of such value and significance. And it did work, for a while. I spent the better part of my paltry savings flying back to Delhi every other weekend, we made plans for the future, he looked at job opportunities in London.

It's difficult to pinpoint when things started to lose their steam. I think when you are in a long-distance relationship there are challenges that at first seem surmountable with good communication and some sacrifices but then those sacrifices start to pinch—you feel like you are missing out on going out or making friends, especially when you are in a new and unfamiliar city, because you have to be home for the nightly 10 p.m. Skype call. When that call and those once eagerly anticipated visits start to feel obligatory you know it's a red flag.

But when you are in a long-distance relationship, it can take all that much longer to realize you are with the wrong person. You spend so little time together and that time is fraught with an almost desperate desire to maximize fun and minimize conflict that much is let go of, swept under the carpet. When I went back to Delhi for ten days during Diwali, I knew that the relationship had lost its sheen. It wasn't just that we had different interests and general attitudes to life or even that we had different priorities—some of my closest friends are happily married to people who are poles apart from them in taste and temperament—it was that we were unable or unwilling to negotiate our differences.

You know you are with the right person when they are able to tolerate inevitable differences between you, and when you in turn can do the same. Unfortunately this realization only hit me when DJ called to tell me he had landed a job with an investment bank in London and could move in a couple of months, around the same time as my internal transfer at Citibank would come through. By then I didn't want the job and I knew then that I didn't want the boy. Upshot? DJ moved to London and I stayed on in Mumbai but left Citibank to embark on a career in films. And no, it didn't end because of my career plans as an actor—we were just not right for each other and when we broke that down, we broke up.

Now, I'm not going to take you through every relationship I've had because I've already covered the ones of note and it really would not serve any purpose other than annoying my husband. Safe to say that when I joined films I had taken to heart my mother's advice not to get involved with an actor, and certainly never to marry one. 'It will complicate your life,' she said to me. 'Actors need a lot of care and attention, they are temperamental, they harbour insecurities, they will either be working too hard or then not at all and both are problematic.' It was good advice—it was true of me and so I knew it was likely to be true of others. So I turned a blind eye to romance. I worked on different films with different people and forged friendships, some temporary—for the duration of the film, such is the nature of the job—but a few that have endured over the years. I was in no hurry to get married or to 'settle down'. The very turn of phrase upset me—there was a reason it was called settle *down* and not settle *up*! I was never one of those women who dreamed of her wedding day from when she was six years old. I had no firm opinions about venue, menu, decor or dress, and as for the groom, I confess there was a mental list, based on experience, not of what I wanted but of what I knew I didn't want.

Not an actor (too much hard work)

Not younger than me (wouldn't be mature enough to 'handle' me)

Not a rigid person with inflexible opinions

Not someone with a big ego

Not possessive or jealous

Not inclined to drama such as slamming doors and kicking furniture

Not someone who has never lived, studied or worked abroad, preferably in England

And not someone with very large feet (that's just always been a personal phobia of mine)

This list didn't include obvious stumbling blocks such as no sense of humour, propensity towards violence, an inability to respect women or cruelty to animals.

Life, as John Lennon famously sang in 'Beautiful Boy', is what happens when you're busy making other plans. It was the spring of 2008 and I had signed a film called *Dhoondte Reh Jaaoge* opposite a young and talented actor. The director wanted us to meet at the Taj Lands End in Bandra for a script reading. They were already seated at the table in the coffee shop when I got there. The director and a well-built boy in straight-fit jeans, a half-sleeved white shirt that barely contained his straining biceps, boots and a belt with a horseshoe bronze buckle. His eyes were hidden behind heavily tinted sunglasses and his hair was a dark mop of unruly curls. My first impression: This boy must live in the gym. What will we talk about on set apart from protein shakes?! It was an opinion that survived well into the shooting of the film because over the course of the Mumbai schedule Kunal must have spoken a total of fifteen words to me.

Made for each other

Far from exchanging numbers, we seemed to steer clear of each other except for when we were in position for a two shot and there was an issue with lighting or camera.

Below are two of the longest conversations we had during those two months:

> Me: So what do you like to do in your spare time?
> Kunal: Not a lot. I like to watch films.
> Me: Do you go out a lot?
> Kunal: No. I like to watch films alone.

End of conversation.

The second took place when I was writing something on my laptop on set:

> Kunal: What are you writing?
> Me: An article for my college, for the *Oxford Magazine*.

End of conversation.

The next day I noticed Kunal had brought a book and was reading intently on set, which was a first. When he was called for a close-up I picked up the thick black leather-bound volume to see what it was. *The Game: Penetrating the Secret Society of Pickup Artists*. There was no conversation between us that day.

I believe there was a force greater than us that wanted us to be together because if the film had not had an outdoor schedule in Malaysia, and if it had not been immediately followed by us having to shoot together in Delhi for another film called *99*, there was no chance of us even forging a friendship, forget embarking on a relationship. We were as different as chalk and cheese, although that idiom doesn't really hold because it implies that I had gotten to know a little bit about who Kunal was. A more apt food product than cheese would be an onion—certainly not in terms of scent or appearance—but in terms of how many layers you have to slowly peel away before you get to his core.

One evening in Langkawi, over eleven games of pool and at least as many cocktails, we got talking and I realized he wasn't dull or indifferent; he was restrained and shy. He wasn't one to be immediately familiar with people; he kept his distance, reserved his attachment and took his time. We stayed up till 6 a.m., talking. He told me stories about growing up in Srinagar, about the exodus, about moving to Mumbai and learning to adjust to a new life, about being a child actor, about his dreams and hopes. I found him fascinating. A life totally different from mine had shaped a person totally different from me. I felt admiration and respect for him. And I was intrigued. I wanted to know him more.

During the course of filming *99* I did get to know him more. And the more I learnt, the more I liked. It didn't hurt that he had these beautiful brown eyes which would dance with equal parts of mischief and innocence, and a lazy lopsided smile that would make me wobbly in the knees—and he used them to full advantage. I haven't read *The Game*, but I can't imagine one can learn to flirt from a book—all he had to do was pin me down with those eyes and my intellectual prowess would be reduced to incoherent babble.

And he was funny. He narrated stories that would leave me doubled over in laughter; he would say and do things that were so uninhibited and entertaining, I couldn't imagine I had once thought him shy. And yet I was acutely aware he was an actor some years younger than me, someone who had not spent much time abroad, and one who was a self-described black-and-white sort of person with zero tolerance for grey. But he did have the most perfectly proportionate feet.

Ours was a courtship dance of nine months with my brain telling me he didn't check all the boxes but my heart rejoicing every time I was in his company.

Ultimately the heart wants what it wants and, in matters of love, you must allow the heart to win. Why Kunal? It wasn't that he was the perfect guy—there's no such thing. The benefit of having had other relationships is that you have the opportunity to comprehend the truth that everyone, even the most initially thrilling prospect, falls short of perfection up close. The more time you spend together the more apparent it is that we are all flawed, we are all broken. It remains to be seen if our broken pieces fit together or if the jagged edges cut too deep.

It will be nine years in June from that evening in Langkawi when our relationship began, as a conversation, one we struggled with at first but have not wanted to close since. A nine-year conversation which we are committed to sustain in perpetuity.

In January of 2015 we decided to solemnize our relationship in an intimate civil marriage at home. To be honest, in our view, the ceremony was superfluous— Kunal and I had already made our promises to each other and truly felt the involvement of the government would not give our bond more sanctity. But it mattered to our families and as it was irrelevant to us—we could just as easily get married as not get married—we decided we might as well get married.

And so in the presence of thirty of our immediate family members we exchanged vows and signed a piece of paper declaring us to be husband and wife.

I am fully aware that marriage is not the only legitimate relationship out there; some go so far as to say that perhaps a partnership of any kind is outdated. A friend of mine insists that the successful relationship paradigm of the future is in fact same-sex non-sexual cohabitation. His most enduring bond has been with his flatmate of six years. They provide for each other in terms of domestic support and personal care, one cooking elaborate meals, the other collating the newest episodes of *Planet Earth* to binge watch. They have some mutual friends and interests

Don't marry the one you can live with,
marry the one you can't live without

and, of course, their own on and off romantic partners, but often holiday apart and don't seem to have any huge expectations from each other. One cannot deny that they seem truly blissful and complication free.

It made me realize that companionship—whether in the form of a husband, a lover, a dog, cat or mongoose, a best friend—is what we all really seek and what we all deserve. I'm all for space, for seclusion and isolation, but not as a way of life.

Marriage is not necessary, but love . . . I would say love is worth the pursuit. Some find it. Those who have less luck keep looking, either whilst determinedly single or while in relationships with those less than ideal. Occasionally they settle for less. If there is one thing that I have learnt that I could impart to those of you who are looking—actively or passively: Don't settle. I know it's sometimes scary being single, especially for those of us who are past the thirty-five-year mark. I know it feels like the later it gets the harder it is to find someone, or at least someone normal, without enough baggage to fill all the lockers at Victoria Terminus. (Are there lockers at VT station? I have never actually been inside!)

And let's not talk about the pressure from family and friends who accuse you of being too picky, too set in your ways—So what if Aditya never remembers your birthday, some boys just aren't good with dates. He doesn't believe you will get that promotion? He's just a realist and doesn't mince his words. Suren only has time for you after 10 p.m.? Perhaps he's just swamped with work, don't nag him! He called you names last night and threw the remote at you? You must have done something to push him over the edge. And the remote didn't actually hit you, right?!

At the end of the day Aditya and Suren are living, breathing men who are willing to marry you. And if you are in your mid to late thirties then you will be constantly reminded of the inevitable passage of time and all the biological decay it brings! Why is it that men produce sperm throughout their lives but we women are born with a finite number of eggs and by the time we are thirty we have lost 90 per cent of them!!

It's enough to scare anyone into a bad marriage! Tick tock boom!

If you haven't already thrown this book across the room and rushed out the door to propose to your Aditya/Suren, I would like to say that, though it may seem like it, it is NOT more important to be in a relationship than to be in a good relationship. With someone who deserves and respects you. With someone who celebrates your achievements, makes an effort with your family, puts you first and tells you at least once a day that they love you. Sure, it's a gamble and there's always the risk that you may not find true love, but when you do, you will find it was worth the wait.

My friend Juhi Pande wrote in the epilogue of her book *Things Your Mother Never Told You About Love*:

Aim for love. Always aim for love. Let the rest be noise.

Because the truth of the matter is that for everything else, there are noise-cancelling headphones.

Worth the Weight

19 March 2017

So I have some news. I can't tell you now, but I can
tell the future you because this book will only be
released at the end of the year and by that time you'll
know already. But for the moment it's our secret.

I'm pregnant!!

Ten weeks and six days to be precise. Another eight
days before we can start telling people.

It's the most difficult secret to keep. Especially from
anyone who knows me even a little bit. How do I explain
the fact that when until now every meal was incomplete
without dessert, even the sight of chocolate makes me
turn green? Or that for someone whose daily exercise—be
it badminton, yoga or the gym—was sacred, I now often
don't have the energy to lift my head off the pillow.

Luckily I'm not a smoker or a big drinker so those
omissions in my diet will not be noticed but the absence

of diet sodas which have pretty much been a staple are sure to raise an eyebrow or two. Oh, and the morning sickness—which, by the way, is not restricted to the morning, but much like the pesky neighbour who doesn't respect boundaries turns up at any moment of the day or night, and lingers. It has been my constant companion for the past three weeks. I have never been on a cruise but I imagine this is what it would feel like—a sustained swell, a continuous churning, a relentless retching. Let's just say it is difficult to disguise.

The other day I ran out of a meeting with the director of a short film I'm doing because the scent of his aftershave made my mouth fill up with water and I had to find a toilet bowl to spit into for ten whole minutes. I have been advised to minimize travel and have had to cancel events two or three weeks in advance with the feeble excuse of illness. What illness that doesn't require hospitalization would afflict you for three weeks!?

Of course by the time this book comes out the future me and the future you will already know how this turns out. But for the moment I'm at sea and I have the sickness to prove it. We've told our immediate families and some of our closest friends—the general advice is not to shout the news from the terrace tops because the first twelve weeks carry the most risk of miscarriage but it would be so difficult to pretend, to go on as normal if the worst were to happen. I think the truth hasn't sunk in as yet for me. There isn't much to see on the outside save the odd zit on my jawline but I am feeling all sorts of things of which fatigue, nausea and indigestion are just some of the more glamorous ones! Today I thought about going for a walk and sat on the bed to tie my shoelaces. I woke up an hour later. Last night I burst into tears because I couldn't decide what to watch on Netflix.

I had intended to spend the month of March writing my chapter on working in films, or falling in love but I can't seem to think about anything else and so I figured I might as well write about this. I am thrilled. I think that's how I knew I wanted to be a mother. Kunal and I had discussed parenthood, of course, but I hadn't really experienced any maternal yearnings and he was in no rush to be a father. So we were in an ambivalent state of not actively planning but also not not-planning. There was pressure; not so much from immediate family—both Kunal's and mine have thankfully always been very liberal and non-conforming in their views—but from others, especially after Kareena and Bhai announced their pregnancy. The media has asked me when I am giving them 'good news'. Random people in lifts have asked me meaningfully how long I have been married. Friends of friends at parties have whispered conspiratorially in my ear about how having a child strengthens a marriage.

The best response I have found is to flick your hair and laugh in their faces while quoting one of the zillion reasons not to add to a burgeoning world population— vomit, poop, stretch marks, cankles and the fact that eventually snuggly cuddly babies ultimately turn into hormonally deranged, obnoxious, know-it-all teenagers.

So when I discovered I was pregnant I wasn't prepared for the involuntary leap of joy my heart took. It was 6 a.m. on 31 January, a time more night than day for me when my senses are as dull as lead. I was only a day late but I am usually as regular as a coffee drinker, if you know what I mean, and so I decided to pee on a stick. As I waited in the bathroom for the pink line or lines to form I caught my reflection in the mirror and held my own gaze. My heart was thudding so loudly in my chest I thought it would wake Kunal who was sleeping in the bedroom some feet away.

There were advantages to either outcome. We loved our life: the freedom to travel at a moment's notice and for any length of time, the intimacy of it just being the two of us at home, the absence of any dependants we had to be responsible for. But if we were going to have a child it should be now. At thirty-eight my gynaecologist had told me about the physical and emotional toll pregnancy takes on an older mother-to-be. The complications and risks that rise exponentially with age. If we delayed too long we ran the risk of things not happening naturally. Whilst there were options down the line like adoption which we were very open to exploring, the question I asked myself in the mirror was, 'Are you ready to be a mother now?'

My question was left hanging unanswered in the air between myself and my reflection. I brought the stick up into my eyeline and there it was. Two pink lines—not faint or shy but bold and unabashed like the legs on a flamingo. I was pregnant. There have been moments in the past when I have been confronted with big news and my reaction has always been consistent. I shut down. Like the time I read on the news ticker at the bottom of the television screen that Bhai had been taken to hospital after an accident. I was sitting at home with friends but they had not noticed the scrolling text across the screen. I continued to sit there unable to move or talk for ten whole minutes until my mother called me on my mobile phone to tell me what I already knew. It was only then that I was jolted into action. Much the same thing happened here. I wrapped the stick in thick reams of toilet paper, hid it in the back of my bedside drawer and went back to sleep. I had read enough to know that a false positive on these things was rare but I think it was too much to process, especially at 6 a.m.

When I woke up a few hours later Kunal was already in the shower. I thought about telling him but then decided I wanted to be absolutely sure first, and so I texted our regular pathology guy Santosh to come home to take a blood sample to test for hCG, the pregnancy hormone. Naturally, when he turned up at 11 a.m. I had to explain his presence to Kunal, which I did rather clumsily, mumbling something about feeling depressed and wanting to check my vitamin D levels. Before he could quiz me further about the sudden onset of this 'depression' I gathered my clothes and locked myself in the bathroom under the pretence of washing my hair for the next twenty minutes.

When I came out he was watching 'best crazy street fights' on YouTube and didn't even notice that my hair was as dry as a bone. We went about our normal routines, including attending an important meeting in Lower Parel with a celebrated director for a film we are co-producing. Although I made all the right noises my mind was on the clock because Santosh had promised to email me the report by 4 p.m. At 4.45 p.m. we were midway through recording some sound bites for a charity fundraiser in support of stray dogs in Mumbai when my phone buzzed. The report had come. I scrolled impatiently through rows of numbers. An hCG level of less than 5 mlIU/ml is considered negative for pregnancy and anything above 25 mlIU/ml is considered positive. And there it was in boldface—hCG 485 mlIU/ml. With video cameras still trained on me as they changed magnification for a close-up, I texted Santosh with trembling fingers.

'What does this mean?' I asked him.

Within seconds his reply came, 'Congratulations, ma'am.'

'Besides starvation and dehydration, stray dogs are also the victims of human cruelty. We appeal to you: Rather than buying a dog from a pet store, please adopt them from animal shelters.'

If you find this video of me online, talking about the hapless condition of strays in India, grinning crazily from ear to ear, you now know why! I couldn't wait to pack the crew off. I took Kunal by the hand to the sofa in our study where, finally, we were all alone. It seemed disloyal that Santosh knew and Kunal did not. At first I just smiled broadly at him, fully expecting him to read the significance of my happiness in my eyes. He looked back at me quizzically at first and then a little nervously. Perhaps he thought my 'depression' had taken a turn for the insane. I would have to use words.

'It's positive!' I exclaimed.

'What is?' he sounded concerned. I suppose because positive on a blood test is so often a bad thing.

'You know . . . the hCG . . . I'm pregnant.' It was so so so weird to say those words aloud and I delivered them like a stilted actor on a film set. I then sat back to take in the effect of this momentous declaration on my poor unsuspecting husband.

I don't know what I expected. Uncertainty. Fear. Panic even. I was mentally prepared to convince him that this was the most beautiful thing to happen to us. What I hadn't prepared for was his complete and unadulterated joy and acceptance.

He didn't even ask me if I was sure, he just pulled me close to him, wrapped his arms around me and said, 'I'm going to the best father in the whole world. I'm going to take him to roller-coaster parks, I'm going to teach him martial arts, I'll have his first drink with him. Or her. Of course. If it's a girl.'

We held each other in silence for a while—a pregnant pause if you will, thinking about what the future held.

'I did a home pregnancy test in the morning,' I whispered into Kunal's neck, 'I didn't tell you because I was scared, but I kept it.'

'I want to see it!' he said. I brought the item in question to him, nestled like a ruby within layers of toilet paper.

We looked at it together in amazement, bewildered by the magnitude of potential behind that small second pink line.

'We should probably throw it away,' Kunal said finally. And we did but not before we took a picture of it.

Think positive

We agreed then that we would not tell anyone except our respective mothers, at least until the first few weeks, fraught with risk and uncertainty, had passed. I was so excited to tell Amman that I dialled her number without even thinking through what I would say. I was imagining how I would now graduate in her eyes from her baby girl to a woman, equal in stature—a mother now too. But in truth I was terrified and clueless and I needed her to soothe me, to tell me that everything would be all right. When I finally told her, she was a reflection of my feelings, mirroring my happiness, my nervousness. Like me she wanted to take things a step at a time, my health being of utmost concern. My mother-in-law was ecstatic. I think deep down she had given up hope of our having a child. She had never prodded me, keeping a discreet distance which I was so grateful for. I felt humbled we could make her so happy. Kunal told me when he gave her the news she fist-pumped as a gesture of victory!

Since then, over six weeks have passed. My life is now divided into weeks, not days or months. I am in my eleventh of forty weeks and the fact that I have a life growing inside me is just about starting to sink in. That is why I can now write about this. We had our first ultrasound in Week 7.

Kunal and I went together feeling giggly and nervous, unsure of what we would see on the inside because there was absolutely nothing to see on the outside.

As I lay on the examining table, Kunal standing beside me clasping my left hand tightly (or was I clasping his?), a grainy black-and-white image popped up on the monitor. I have to confess I couldn't make any sense of it and the doctor had to point out the little blob in the middle of my uterus—the embryo, our baby! And there it was . . . in the centre of the embryo—a heartbeat measuring 135 beats a minute. If ever there was a reality check, this was it. A single live intrauterine pregnancy of seven weeks.

We have told a few more people since: siblings, close friends without whom this journey would feel incomplete anyway.

In fact a spooky thing happened the other day, which prompted us to spill the beans to Bhai and Kareena. I woke up to a text message from her which said: 'I had a dream that you're pregnant. Please check.'

WEIRD. I poked Kunal in the ribs to wake him up so he could read it too. 'Maybe she has a new maternal sixth sense or something,' he mumbled sleepily.

I wrote back some fluff about how a dream about being pregnant actually symbolized something much deeper and that perhaps she was suddenly feeling a closer connection to me which I was very appreciative of. There was no reply.

Only a few hours later, as we were returning home from a lunch we stopped at a traffic light under a bridge.

There was a massive hoarding of Kareena holding a PregaNews home pregnancy test and saying, *'Aaj mujhe good news mili.'* It was a sign, literally.

And so we told them.

We told Kunal's father. We told my sister and Kunal's sister. Of course, everyone is thrilled—we *are* married and over sixteen—but the funniest reaction was my brother's. He looked . . . relieved.

'Thank God,' he exclaimed, slapping his hand on his forehead. 'Now you guys can take Taimur and your child to Disneyland and play football with them and do all the things I'm too old to do! And then they can come to me for a bedtime story.' He was so genuinely reassured it was endearing.

As time passes, feelings of excitement and bliss abound, of course, but the prevailing emotion is anxiety. It is my responsibility to carry this miracle to a safe and healthy birth; sustaining this pregnancy is now the single most important goal of my life. Along the way there are multiple milestones, each a significant marker of the baby's well-being—anomaly scans, genetic screenings, blood tests . . . Everyone tells me to be positive but it is hard to shake the fear that my child will be born less than perfect—I'm sure this is something all expecting mothers experience. My friend in Chicago who has had three healthy babies reminded me that worrying for your children is part and parcel of being a parent and it most certainly doesn't end with birth. Most children are born healthy and survive a multitude of early injuries and illnesses. In fact she half-joked that the greatest threat to their existence is the very real chance we will kill them ourselves when they are teenagers! As irrational as these fears may be I will feel a huge sense of relief when the results of the tests are in and are clear.

~

13 April 2017

It's now three weeks and four days later—Week 14, Day 3—and I am officially in my second trimester.

As I read these last few pages I am amused by the level of minutiae I have chosen to share with all of you who are now no doubt feeling like you have strayed into a pregnancy chat room. The good news is all the tests are clear and it is finally starting to sink in that this is happening. And I'm starting to show!

I was shooting for the National Spelling Bee which I host every year and my stylist sourced the usual petite-sized clothing for me—which included a high-waisted pair of black trousers and a red crop top. I could just about zip up the pants but I almost passed out from having to

Baby shower, girl power

Does the balloon make my
bump look smaller?

When Taimur met Masti

Showered with love

hold in my stomach all day! Definitely time to invest in some elastic waistbands.

It won't just be my size and shape that will change, hopefully only temporarily. This marks a new chapter

Did you say you're glowing or you're growing?

for Kunal and me—we are going to be parents with a capital P for permanent. The truth of the matter is that I have been so focused on being pregnant—basking in the glow of impending motherhood, graciously accepting people's blessings and good wishes, soaking up all the attention I am owed for my crucial role in the miracle of creation, flaunting my bump in my new maternity wardrobe, planning my artistically tasteful pregnant photo shoot—that I had forgotten all about how this ends. With a baby! I am aware that life as I know it will never be the same again—people have told me so enough times—but I remain a little foggy about what exactly that means.

'Get as much sleep as you can now' has been the most frequently given advice and I have taken it to heart, sleeping a minimum of ten hours a night. But you can't bank sleep in advance, you know. You can make up for an all-nighter spent partying or working by napping through the day or sleeping in the next morning but it doesn't work the same way when you're trying to store sleep for future sleepless nights. The thought of not sleeping through the night or having to wake up at 6 a.m. without commensurate monetary compensation for the same is an entirely alien one.

Anyone who has been through the experience of childbirth seems to want to share their wisdom with an expecting mother. Be it delivery: 'You must try for a natural birth because the recovery is much quicker. I was home the same day and back in the gym two weeks later' and 'Opt for an elective C-section if you want to have a semblance of a happy marriage post birth. Labour is primitive and outdated'. Nursing: 'You must breastfeed as breast milk is a perfect cocktail of vitamins, protein and fat. You will also burn extra calories and bond with your child better' and 'Infant formula has all the nutrients your baby needs, your husband can also feed the baby and feel involved and it's so much more convenient so you can have a life of your own which is essential.' Rocking: 'Let the baby cry itself to sleep or it will be a whiny needy cling-on' and 'Babies need to be held and are soothed by the touch of your skin so hold them and rock them to sleep as often as you can.' It can be overwhelming—all that well-meaning, contradictory advice.

The best advice I have got to date is from my friend in London who has two beautiful baby girls: Listen politely, smile and nod, remember what makes sense to you and flush the rest down a mental toilet.

If there is one thing I struggle with it's the question of whether having a career after becoming a mother, especially through your child's early years, is a good or bad thing. There is a lot of passive if not outspoken judgement about this, with lobbyists on both sides taking up their cause with equal passion and belief. I can only speak from experience: My mother was a working mother and I have vivid memories of watching her get ready for work in the morning. There were also long spells when she was away from us for outdoor shoots. My father on the other hand was a retired professional sportsman and was consequently home a lot. Growing up I never realized this was an unusual dynamic, especially in India. We were proud of Amman's success and drew inspiration from it. We were witness to my father's unflinching support and we respected him for it.

Of course, we missed her—there were school plays, sports days and even the odd birthday that she was unable to attend, although she would have tried her best to be there, but we waited to celebrate with her when she was back. I had a happy, stable childhood and trite as it may sound my mother continues to be my role model even today. My desire to be independent comes from her as does my work ethic and my sense of commitment to my career.

Women, be it stay-at-home mothers or working ones, face flak either way for their choices. Either they are criticized for taking it too easy by quitting their jobs to raise their children and manage the household (anyone who thinks being a full-time parent is easy clearly doesn't know which way is up!) or they are censured for pursuing a career and therefore devoting attention that should go to the child to their own selfish ambitions. As the daughter of a working mother, and as someone who certainly intends to work after my child is born, I resent these judgements and stigmas. I believe it is possible to be good at both your job and motherhood because my own mother did just that. She may not have 'needed' to financially provide for her family but she wanted to contribute and she wanted to follow her passion and she didn't need to justify her reasons to anyone.

My father was never asked who was looking after the children when he was commentating at a cricket match or playing third umpire, so why should my mother, Kareena, or any other working mother be asked the same. Women's empowerment may not be a reality as yet but the more we support women choosing their place—be it in the home or at work—the closer we come to that ideal.

What will *my* place of choice be? I don't want to commit myself to something right now but I imagine I will continue to want to act in films, produce content, perhaps even write another book or I may venture into a whole new area such as teaching or soap-making—as long as it's something of my own that excites and drives me. I don't want to be that woman who turns around at the age of fifty and resents her child or husband for usurping her identity and her dreams.

I hope one day my child will read this book—this book that I started writing before she was even conceived, but as soon as I knew she was growing inside me, bigger and stronger with each passing day, it dawned on me that I was always writing it for her. They say that to instil a love of books you should start reading to your child while it is still in the womb. Here I am, writing to mine.

I hope that through this book she will learn about and take pride in her family and their achievements; discover things about me and my childhood and certainly about an era of nawabs and begums, of tradition and ceremony that is all but gone; and know how exhilarated and humbled both her parents were to learn of her miraculous existence.

Above all I hope that she will learn that it doesn't matter if she chooses a public or private life; if she becomes an actor, athlete, activist or stay-at-home mother; if she becomes famous—moderately or outrageously—or not. What matters is that she is where she wants to be and that she is happy.

Introducing Inaaya

Acknowledgements

T his book would not have been possible if it weren't
      for my family because of whom I am who I am, and
quite frankly because of whom there was some interest in
my writing a book in the first place.

This book would not have been written if it weren't
for my agents Anjali and Shvate who convinced me to
write it and the good people at Penguin Random House
who sought to publish it.

This book would never have been finished if it wasn't
for my husband, Kunal, who stood beside me and watched
over me (often literally) until it was done—you are quite
simply my reason for being.

I must thank the following people for taking
the time and effort to read drafts of this book and for
providing invaluable critical feedback, most of which I

have absorbed—Kunal, my mother, my brother, Saif, my editor, Gurveen, and my friends Navraaz, Priyanka, Ninna, Sanyuktha, Shweta, Amrit and Nayan.

Thank you, Tom, for being the hero of my chapter on travel.

Finally, I would like to thank Shantanu Ray Chaudhuri for translating the two poems by Tagore into English.